The Expository Pulpit Series

GALATIANS

Liberated For Living

by

Dr. Glen Spencer Jr.

GLEN SPENCER JR.
15 Pine Ridge Road – Tunkhannock, Pa. 18657

Phone:. (570) 333-4263 –Email: GraceForLiving@epix.net

Galatians: Liberated For Living
Copyright © 2011 by Glen Spencer Jr.

All Rights Reserved. No part of this book may be reproduced, stored in a retrieval system or transmitted in any form by any means, electronic, mechanical, photocopy, recording, or otherwise, without the prior permission of the author, except as provided by USA copyright law.

Contents

Paul's Greeting 9

There's Only One True Gospel 15

The Gospel Will Change Your Life 19

The Issue Has Already Been Settled 25

In Defense Of The Gospel 31

Crucified With Christ 39

Bewitched 45

Abraham And The Gospel 53

God's Schoolmaster 63

Coming Of Age 75

The Pitfalls Of Legalism 87

Liberty Or Slavery 97

Living In Liberty 101

The War Within 113

The Works Of The Flesh 123

The Fruit Of The Spirit 133

The Ministry Of Restoration 157

The Harvest Is Coming 163

Glorying In The Cross 167

Recommendations From Our Readers

Pastor Spencer is not only a gifted preacher, but a gifted writer as well. As a fundamentalist and pastor, I am careful about the books I endorse, but Dr. Spencer is at the top of my list of writers. So, it is with great honor that I recommend his Expository Pulpit Series to you.

Michael D. McClary, Th.D,
Pastor, Community-Bainbridge Baptist Church,
Founder/Executive Director, Good Samaritan Ministries

I have enjoyed reading your books in the past and look forward to getting newer ones. The thing I enjoyed about your books were that when I read them I said, "I have to teach this to my people. I want others to know this". I appreciate your study, work and insight.

Dr. Jeff Fugate
Pastor, Clays Mill Road Baptist Church
President of Commonwealth Baptist College

Dr. Glen Spencer's Bible commentaries are valuable for today. They are expository, edifying and exciting in aiding the Christian, the teacher and the preacher to understand the mind of God and to become victorious in their daily lives. I will use the complete set.

Dr. Bruce Miller, Evangelist
President of Atlantic Coast Baptist College

It is with great delight that I recommend to you, "The Expository Pulpit Commentary Series." Dr. Glen Spencer Jr. combines years of exhaustive research and practical ministry experience to bring to the church, the pastor, the teacher, and the student of the Scriptures a sound, in-depth and yet very practical set of study tools. This ongoing verse by commentary series will be a great addition to your library. This is not just more rehashed information but wise insight from a seasoned Bible Scholar. I know Dr. Glen Spencer Jr. the man and have found him to be a great Christian, a compassionate pastor and a true champion of the authorized King James Bible, believing it to be God's Preserved Word For English speaking people.

This trustworthy commentary series is, Dispensational in theology, pre-Tribulation and pre-millennial in its eschatology, literal in its hermeneutical approach and expository in its format. I am thrilled that this good work is now available to you and I as we seek to benefit from its invaluable help to deepen our knowledge of God's perfect, preserved word.

Dr. Jon M. Jenkins,
Pastor, Grace Baptist Church
President of Grace Baptist College

"You have written an excellent study on the Book of Revelation. This will be a great help to preachers and teachers everywhere. This work is informative, inspiring, and encouraging. Your alliterative outlines are excellent! Your study of this book will be a great help to many, many Christians."

Dr. Lee Roberson
Founder of Tennessee Temple University

Introduction

The Place Of The Letter

Galatia was a province in the southern region of Asia Minor. It is modern day Turkey. This region was comprised of Iconium, Lystra, and Debre. Paul visited Galatia twice, once while on his second missionary journey (Acts 16:6) and again on his third missionary journey (Acts 18:23).

The People Of The Letter

The Galatians were Gauls, a nation of barbarians who invaded Greece in the third century before Christ. These Gauls were conquered by the Romans in 189 B.C. and became the province Galatia.

The Purpose Of The Letter

The reason for this letter was to correct error in the churches of Galatia. The Judaizers had infiltrated the Galatian Church with their teachings, attempting to mix law with grace and faith with works. These false teachers had convinced the Galatians that they could not be saved by faith in Christ alone, but had to both believe in Christ and keep the law to be saved and remain saved. As a result, many of the Galatian believers had become victims of Legalism. So, Paul sets the record straight, setting forth and defending the pure gospel of Jesus Christ.

The Authentication of the Gospel (Chapters 1-2)

The Affirmation of the Gospel (Chapters 3-4)

The Application of the Gospel (Chapters 5-6)

The Problems Of The Letter

There were two prevailing problems that stand out in Galatians. 1) There was the question of Paul's apostleship. Paul also had to deal with the same issue with the Corinthian Church. 2) Due to the Judaizers Paul had to deal extensively with the doctrine of salvation.

The Premise Of The Letter

Few books have had a more powerful impact on the Church as the book of Galatians. This book has been called "The Charter Of Freedom," "The Christian Declaration Of Independence," and "The Magna Carta of Christian Liberty."

Subjected Outline

The Foundation of our Liberty (Chapters 1-2)

The Features of our Liberty (Chapters 3-4)

The Fulfillment of our Liberty (Chapters 5-6)

Paul's Greeting
Galatians 1:1-5

The book of Galatians is called the "Christian's Declaration of Independence." Paul teaches and clearly establishes the fact that the Christian is free from the curse and bondage of the Law. After introducing himself, He powerfully argues the doctrine of justification by faith.

PAUL'S MANDATE

Paul, an apostle, (not of men, neither by man, but by Jesus Christ, and God the Father, who raised him from the dead;) (Galatians 1:1) Paul begins this letter with a dogmatic declaration that he is **an apostle...** The word **apostle** means *"a sent one"* and carries the idea of a commissioned emissary or messenger. Paul became an apostle when he encountered the Lord Jesus Christ on the Damascus road (Acts 9). Paul preached the gospel pure and straight just as it was given to him. He preached that Jesus Christ is the one and only Saviour. He preached faith in Christ apart from works (Acts 16:31, Ephesians 2:8-9). The legalists came in after Paul's departure and began mixing law with grace and faith with works. These false teachers had convinced many of the Galatians that they could not be saved by faith in Christ alone, but had to both believe in Christ and keep the law to be saved and remain saved. One of their methods of promoting their false doctrine was to question Paul's apostleship and authority claiming that he was not a genuine apostle. They figured that if they could question and discredit Paul's apostleship, they could cast doubt on his message. This is the old philosophy of attacking the messenger if you don't like the message.

From the start Paul identifies himself as an Apostle. He makes it clear that his apostleship was **... not of men, neither by man, but by Jesus Christ, and God the Father...** Paul wanted it clearly understood that he was God's apostle. He wasn't sent by man or momma. He was God's man sent by God and no other.

PAUL'S MANNERISM

Grace be to you and peace from God the Father, and from our Lord Jesus Christ, (Galatians 1:3) Paul's message was a comforting one. He starts out with **Grace be to you and peace...** This greeting is characteristic of Paul's letter. Take note that grace and peace are **from God the Father, and from our Lord Jesus Christ.** There is no other source of true grace and peace. **Grace** is the thing that the world needs the most and **peace** is the thing that she seeks the most.

The Extending Of Grace

Grace is God's unmerited favor toward us. Grace is God doing for us that which we cannot do for ourselves—it is God's loving favor to the unworthy. Grace is God's loving favor toward those who deserve His judgment. **But God commendeth his love toward us, in that, while we were yet sinners, Christ died for us. (Romans 5:8)** We are described as sinners and sinners must die for their sin. God had declared, **The soul that sinneth, it shall die ... (Ezekiel 18:20)** Death is the natural result of sin. James said, **... sin,**

when it is finished, bringeth forth death. (James 1:15)** Not only are we sinners, but in our lost condition we were enemies of God. Paul said, **...when we were enemies, we were reconciled to God by the death of his Son... (Romans 5:10)** When we were hopeless and helpless God offered grace and sent Jesus Christ to die for our sin. As awful as sin is with all of it depravity and destruction, it is no match for the grace of God. The Scriptures assure us that **... where sin abounded, grace did much more abound: (Romans 5:20)**

The Experience Of Peace

Peace is the result of having experienced the grace of God. There can be no real or lasting peace without God's grace and mercy. There is a false peace that this world searches for, but to no avail. **For when they shall say, Peace and safety; then sudden destruction cometh upon them, as travail upon a woman with child; and they shall not escape. (1 Thessalonians 5:3)** Politicians and peace talks do not bring peace to a weary soul. They might be able to negotiate a cease fire, but even after the bombs stop exploding and the rifles lie in silence, the war rages on in the soul. Where God's grace has not transformed the heart there is no real peace. The world knows nothing of this kind of peace and joy. **There is no peace, saith the LORD, unto the wicked. (Isaiah 48:22)** Paul spoke of a peace that only a believer can experience. **Therefore being justified by faith, we have peace with God through our Lord Jesus Christ: By whom also we have access by faith into this grace wherein we stand, and rejoice in hope of the glory of God. (Romans 5:1-2)** You say, *"How is it possible to experience such peace in this wicked word?"* Jesus answered that question when He said, **These things I have spoken unto you, that in me ye**

might have peace. In the world ye shall have tribulation: but be of good cheer; I have overcome the world. (John 16:33) Our peace comes as a result of Christ's victory over the world.

PAUL'S MESSAGE

Who gave himself for our sins, that he might deliver us from this present evil world, according to the will of God and our Father: (Galatians 1:4) Paul's message was powerful and effective. Everywhere he went he preached the gospel of Christ. Even in his salutation to the Galatians he got the gospel in. Look at Paul's message:

The Sacrifice Of The Message

Who gave himself... (Galatians 1:4a) If there is to be salvation there must be an acceptable sacrifice. Here is the summit of the salvation message. Jesus Christ **gave himself** as a sacrifice for lost mankind.

> **For there is one God, and one mediator between God and men, the man Christ Jesus; Who gave himself a ransom for all, to be testified in due time. (1 Timothy 2:5-6)**

> **Looking for that blessed hope, and the glorious appearing of the great God and our Saviour Jesus Christ; Who gave himself for us, that he might redeem us from all iniquity, and purify unto himself a peculiar people, zealous of good works. (Titus 2:13-14)**

Sacrifice speaks of death and blood and reminds us of the awful suffering and shame that Christ endured to be our Saviour. He literally **gave himself** for us. This is what He came for. Like the sacrificial lamb of the Old Testament, Christ shed His blood for our sins. **In whom we have redemption through his blood, even the forgiveness of sins. (Colossians 1:14)** When John The Baptist saw Jesus he said, **Behold the Lamb of God, which taketh away the sin of the world. (John 1:29)** Lost man could do nothing to satisfy the righteous demands of God. Divine justice could only be satisfied by a Divine sacrifice. Divine mercy could only be secured by the payment of a Divine price. Thank God! We have both in Jesus Christ who suffered the wrath of Almighty God in our place.

The Substitute Of The Message

... for our sins (Galatians 1:b) Let us never forget that it was our sin that nailed Christ to the cross of Calvary. He was innocent. He knew no sin. He was perfectly righteous and holy. He died as a substitute for our sin. **For he hath made him to be sin for us, who knew no sin; that we might be made the righteousness of God in him. (2 Corinthians 5:21)** As Jesus hung on the cross He took upon Himself the sins of the whole world. He died vicariously as our substitute. **And he is the propitiation for our sins: and not for ours only, but also for the sins of the whole world. (1 John 2:2)**

The Salvation Of The Message

... that he might deliver us from this present evil world, (Galatians 1:4c) Notice that the world is described as evil. John said, **... the whole world lieth in wickedness. (1 John 5:19)** This world is under Satan's influence. He is called **...the god of this world. (2 Corinthians 4:4)** It is driven by wickedness and runs contrary to the laws and nature of God and is at enmity with Him. Lost man is a natural product of this world. Apart from Christ man is a slave of his depravity and hopelessly bound to this world system. But look again! Christ died **that he might deliver us from this present evil world.** The word **deliver** carries the idea of being rescued. When there was no way out, no escape, no hope, Christ paid the price and rescued us from the clutches of sin and set us free.

The Sovereignty Of The Message

... according to the will of God and our Father: To whom be glory for ever and ever. Amen. (Galatians 1:4d-5) Of course, the work of Christ was according to the will of God. Imagine this! It is God's will that the lost be saved.

> **But as many as received him, to them gave he power to become the sons of God, even to them that believe on his name: Which were born, not of blood, nor of the will of the flesh, nor of the will of man, but of God. (John 1:12-13)**

> **The Lord is not slack concerning his promise, as some men count slackness; but is longsuffering to us-ward, not willing that any should perish, but that all should come to repentance. (2 Peter 3:9)**

The Holy God of glory, despite my sinful condition, loved me and wanted to bring me into the family of God and fellowship with me.

There's Only One True Gospel
Galatians 1:6-9

In most of Paul's letters, we find some praise of the recipients, before dealing with the subject of the letter. Paul didn't do that here. He immediately jumps into the matter at hand. When the gospel is at stake there is no time for pleasantries. The issue must be dealt with.

THE GALATIANS WHO WERE REMOVED

I marvel that ye are so soon removed from him that called you into the grace of Christ unto another gospel: (Galatians 1:6) The believer's at Galatia had accepted doctrine that was contrary to the gospel of Jesus Christ. Paul was astonished at their failure to hold the line on what they had been taught as well as their accepting the false teachings of the Judaizers.

The Apostasy at Galatia

The word **removed** comes from *"metatithaymee"* and means *"to change, remove, fall away, desert, turn away from someone, changing sides."* That is exactly what many of the Galatian believers had done! They had fallen away from the truth and changed their doctrine. They had turned away from Christ and sided with the Judaizers. They had actually apostatized. The Galatians had actually turned their back on Christ, His truth and Paul.

The Amazement Of Paul

Paul said, **I marvel that ye are so soon removed...** The word **marvel** comes from *"thaumazo"* and means *"to be* *astonished or amazed."* Paul was amazed at just how quickly the Galatians could be persuaded to change sides. This was no small matter! It was the **grace of Christ** that they had rejected and removed themselves from. No wonder Paul stood in amazement. At first they had readily and enthusiastically received the gospel of the grace of God from Paul. Paul spoke of their reception of the gospel of grace when he said, **... for I bear you record, that, if it had been possible, ye would have plucked out your own eyes, and have given them to me. (Galatians 4:15)** They were so appreciative of Paul and his message that they would have done anything for him. Now they have rejected the whole package and embraced a works and law mixture that Paul described as perverted.

Paul was amazed that the Galatians were **soon removed.** It didn't take long for the Judaizers to dupe and derail them. In the short amount of time between Paul giving them the gospel and the Judaizers coming into their Church, the Galatians rejected the true gospel and embraced false doctrine moving away from grace and freedom and into legalism and bondage. It is amazing even in our day how quickly folks will listen to false teachers and embrace their false doctrine.

THE GRACE THAT WAS REJECTED

The Galatians had been called into the **grace of Christ** but the Judaizers had succeeded in leading them to abandon salvation by grace and embrace **another gospel: (Galatians 1:6)** There are issues that we can disagree on and still get along and move forward for the cause of Christ. However, when it comes to the message of the gospel of the grace of

God there is no middle ground. There can be no compromise. Because they had attempted to mix grace with the law and faith with works they had abandoned the true gospel and embraced what Paul calls **another gospel.**

THE GOSPEL THAT WAS REDUCED

Which is not another; but there be some that trouble you, and would pervert the gospel of Christ. (Galatians 1:7) The gospel is the very foundation of the Christian faith. When a man hears the message of salvation and embraces that message by placing faith in Jesus Christ, he is banking his eternal destiny on it. Changing the message of the gospel of the grace of God results in sidetracking souls for whom Christ died. To change anything about the gospel is to pervert it. In verse 6 when Paul talked about **another** gospel he used the word *"heteros,"* meaning *"one of a different kind."* Here in verse 7 he uses the Greek word *allos*, meaning, *"one of the same kind."* They were removed from the gospel of the grace of God and embraced another Gospel that was not the same kind. When the message is changed in any way it is no longer the same and it is no longer the gospel of the grace of God. Their new theology was different in its very nature from God's gospel of grace. They could call it the gospel of Christ, but by its very nature it was not the gospel of Christ. It had been changed. It was another of a different kind. The Galatians had abandoned liberty for legalism.

THE GUILTY THAT WERE REBUKED

But though we, or an angel from heaven, preach any other gospel unto you than that which we have preached unto you, let him be accursed. As we said before, so say I

now again, **If any man preach any other gospel unto you than that ye have received, let him be accursed. (Galatians 1:8-9)** So serious is this matter that Paul pronounces a curse on the Judaizers and then immediately repeats himself. Twice he says anyone who preaches another gospel, **let him be accursed.** The word **accursed** comes from *anathema*. It speaks of a person who is without hope and doomed to destruction. When another gospel which is not another gospel is preached it has the curse of God on it and the individual who preaches it. You will notice that Paul excluded no one from this curse. He said, **though we, or an angel from heaven, preach any other gospel ... If any man...** There were no exclusions! If it were himself, anyone else or even an angel from Heaven, if they preached another gospel, they were doomed and without hope.

The Gospel Will Change Your Life
Galatians 1:10-24

You will remember that in his opening remarks Paul defended his apostleship against those who had tried to discredit him (Galatians 1:10). After describing the work of the gospel (Galatians 1:4), he then pronounced a divine curse on anyone who would distort the gospel of grace (Galatians 1:6-9). In the remainder of chapter 1 he once again takes up the issue of his authority and messages, defending himself against the false charges of his critics.

PAUL'S PRIORITY

For do I now persuade men, or God? or do I seek to please men? for if I yet pleased men, I should not be the servant of Christ. (Galatians 1:10) Paul wasn't competing in a popularity contest. He had one motive and that was to please the Lord. Paul knew that it was impossible to please both man and God. There is no middle ground when it comes to serving Christ. He must come first. Jesus said, **No man can serve two masters ... (Matthew 6:24)** Paul never played politics. He never sought to bring honor himself. His desire was to magnify and honor his Lord.

PAUL'S PREACHING

But I certify you, brethren, that the gospel which was preached of me is not after man. For I neither received it of man, neither was I taught it, but by the revelation of Jesus Christ. (Galatians 1:11-12) Paul received his call and commission by Divine revelation. His message did not come from man or school. The origin of the gospel is God Himself.

Man was not involved in presenting the gospel to Paul. God met Paul personally on the Damascus road and it was by Divine revelation that Paul became personally acquainted with the Saviour. Paul said, **... For I neither received it of man, neither was I taught it, but by the revelation of Jesus Christ.** When Paul said **who art thou, Lord?** and the answer came back, **... I am Jesus whom thou persecutest. (Acts 9:5),** Paul realized that Jesus Christ was Lord of glory. It was there that he was **<u>Converted</u>**, **<u>Called</u>** and **<u>Commissioned</u>**.

PAUL'S PROOF

Having been challenged so far as his authority and message, Paul calls their attention to what he was before Christ changed his life. The evidence was indisputable! A major change had taken place in Paul. When Peter and John were brought before Caiaphas and his crowd for preaching the gospel and healing the lame man; Caiaphas and his boys got their heads together, **Saying, What shall we do to these men? for that indeed a notable miracle hath been done by them is manifest to all them that dwell in Jerusalem; and we cannot deny it. (Acts 4:16)** They could argue with their theology. They could argue with their methods of ministry. But they couldn't argue the results. The same was true of Paul. His life served as a clear illustration of the power of the gospel. His life was proof that the gospel worked. Notice three thoughts as Paul gives his testimony.

<u>Paul's Profit in the Jew's Religion</u>

For ye have heard of my conversation in time past in the Jews' religion ... And profited in the Jews' religion above many my equals in mine own nation, being more exceedingly zealous of the traditions of my fathers.

(Galatians 1:13a, 14) The word **conversation** speaks of *"behavior, conduct or manner of life."* It carries the idea of lifestyle. Not what one says with their lips, but what their life says. Paul had an impressive reputation when it came to his religion.

Paul testified that he **...profited in the Jews' religion above many my equals in mine own nation.** The word **profited (14)** means *"to advance, drive forward, or to increase."* He says, **... being more exceedingly zealous of the traditions of my fathers.** Paul was zealous and committed concerning his religion. Few men excelled as Paul did.

> **Circumcised the eighth day, of the stock of Israel, *of* the tribe of Benjamin, an Hebrew of the Hebrews; as touching the law, a Pharisee; Concerning zeal, persecuting the church; touching the righteousness which is in the law, blameless. (Philippians 3:5-6)**

Paul excelled in his religion. But religion is all it was. It was a Pharisaical system of dead religion and self-righteousness that accomplished nothing so far as Paul's real need of salvation was concerned.

Paul's Persecution of the Church

Paul goes on to say, **...how that beyond measure I persecuted the church of God, and wasted it: (Galatians 1:13b)** Webster defines **persecution** as meaning, *"harassed by troubles or punishments unjustly inflicted, particularly for religious opinions."* Paul was a militant legalist who despised with vengeance anyone who would name the name of Christ. The word **wasted** comes from *portheo* and means

"to waste, to ravage, to destroy." The idea is that of plundering a defeated city. Paul's desire and intent was to completely eradicate the Church. This is what he lived for.

Paul testified that ...**beyond measure** [he] **persecuted the church of God, and wasted it.** Paul is first mentioned in Acts 8, where, as Saul, he participated in the execution of Stephen, the first martyr. **And Saul was consenting unto his death. And at that time there was a great persecution against the church which was at Jerusalem; and they were all scattered abroad throughout the regions of Judaea and Samaria, except the apostles. (Acts 8:1)** The word **consenting** means to *"think well of, assent to, feel gratified with, assent, be pleased, have pleasure in."* So caught up was Paul in his religion and persecution of the Church that he actually felt gratified and pleased at the stoning of Stephen. The tense of the words **persecuted** and **wasted** indicate that this was a continual way of life for Paul. He lived to persecute the Church (Acts 8:3, 9:21; 22:3-5,19-20; 26:10,11; 1 Timothy 1:12-13). Jesus said, **... the time cometh, that whosoever killeth you will think that he doeth God service. (John 16:2)** Paul was convinced that he was actually doing God's work by persecuting the Church.

Paul's Preaching of the Gospel

But when it pleased God, who separated me from my mother's womb, and called me by his grace, To reveal his Son in me, that I might preach him among the heathen; (Galatians 1:15b-16a) Paul's testimony moves from religions emptiness to Christ's salvation and calling. The word **separated** is used several times in connection with Paul's call into the ministry. Paul said to the Romans that he was ... **called to be an apostle, separated unto the gospel of God,**

(Romans 1:1) At Antioch the Holy Spirit said, **... Separate me Barnabas and Saul for the work whereunto I have called them. (Acts 13:2)** The word **separated** means to *"set off by boundary or divide."* God had set boundaries in Paul's life. Paul said, **... To reveal his Son in me, that I might preach him among the heathen.** The idea is that Paul was called of God to live and serve within the parameter and boundary of the gospel ministry.

Paul said, **...immediately I conferred not with flesh and blood: (Galatians 1:16b)** The word **conferred** carries the idea of consulting. Paul's calling was clear. He didn't check to see if man approved. His concern was to please his Saviour. In his letter to the Corinthian Church Paul expressed the importance of his call. **For though I preach the gospel, I have nothing to glory of: for necessity is laid upon me; yea, woe is unto me, if I preach not the gospel! (1 Corinthians 9:16)** Notice that phrase, ... **for necessity is laid upon me.** This was a Divine compulsion to preach the Word of God. He had been apprehended by God, and the compulsion was such that he had no choice but to preach the gospel. Paul didn't need man's permission, he had God's call.

Neither went I up to Jerusalem to them which were apostles before me; but I went into Arabia, and returned again unto Damascus. (Galatians 1:17) Paul's argument is that if he was in Arabia and Damascus for three years, then he wasn't in Jerusalem being taught his doctrine by the Apostles. His Apostleship and message was solely dependent upon Jesus Christ.

Then after three years I went up to Jerusalem to see Peter, and abode with him fifteen days. But other of the

apostles saw I none, save James the Lord's brother. Now the things which I write unto you, behold, before God, I lie not. (Galatians 1:18-20) Only after spending three years in Arabia and Damascus did Paul go to Jerusalem. Paul's argument is that he had been preaching the gospel, winning folks to Christ, and training converts for three years before he ever went to Jerusalem and met Peter. Even then, Paul only stayed **fifteen days.** Hardly enough time to be trained in a new ministry. Paul received his apostleship and his message from God, not from others.

Afterwards I came into the regions of Syria and Cilicia; And was unknown by face unto the churches of Judaea which were in Christ: (Galatians 1:21-22) The record bore witness that Paul was busy for Christ in other places. He couldn't have been trained and indoctrinated by the Apostles in Jerusalem during this period if he was preaching the gospel and planting churches in Syria and Cilicia.

Paul contends that he was **unknown by face unto the churches of Judaea.** He had never been to Judaea. Therefore they didn't even know what Paul looked like.

But they had heard only, That he which persecuted us in times past now preacheth the faith which once he destroyed. And they glorified God in me. (Galatians 1:23-24) They had never seen but they had heard of him. The man who had once made it the business of his life to stamp out Christian's was now just as committed to spreading of message. The story of Paul's conversion to Christ had preceded him and those who heard the news glorified God for it.

The Issue Has Already Been Settled
Galatians 2:1-10

After having established in chapter one that his salvation and apostleship was by direct revelation from Jesus Christ, Paul points out that the issue of grace and works had already been settled. There are only two religions in the world today. They operate under many names, sects and denominations, but they still fall into one of two categories. They either believe in salvation by works, or salvation by grace. A sinner is either saved by grace or he is saved by works. Either salvation is a gift or it is something we earn. There can be no mixture of the two. These systems are direct opposites

THE JERUSALEM CONFERENCE

Paul begins to set forth and defend the truth that salvation is only by grace through faith in the Lord Jesus Christ.

The Season of the Conference

Then fourteen years after I went up again to Jerusalem with Barnabas, and took Titus with me also. (Galatians 2:1) There is quite a bit of debate over the exact time of this particular visit to Jerusalem. In the book of Acts we find that Paul made a total of five trips to Jerusalem.

1. His first trip was from Damascus (Acts 9:26-30).
2. The visit in which Paul and Barnabas took a famine relief gift to the church at Jerusalem (Acts 11:27-30; 12:24–25).

3. The Jerusalem Council visit (Acts 15:1-30).

4. The visit at the end of his second missionary journey (Acts 18:21-22).

5. Then there was his final visit (Acts 21:15-23:35).

Since the subject of Galatians 2 parallels Act 15, it would stand to reason that it is the Jerusalem Council trip that Paul has in mind here.

The Sanction of the Conference

And I went up by revelation... (Galatians 2:2a) Paul now takes his readers to the Jerusalem Council (Acts 15). Paul said, **I went up by revelation.** Paul's trip to Jerusalem was not the result of his own desires, neither was it because of a summons from the Jerusalem council. It was by direct revelation of God that Paul made this journey to Jerusalem.

The Subject of the Conference

... and communicated unto them that gospel which I preach among the Gentiles, (Galatians 2:2b) Paul stated the subject of the council **that gospel which I preach.** The issue at the Jerusalem council was the same issue that Paul was facing in Galatia. The question of law and grace had already been settled by the Jerusalem Church. Their conclusion was that the gospel was to be preached to the Gentiles without any mixture of the law. It was to be the pure unadulterated gospel of God's grace.

The Selection of the Conference

... but privately to them which were of reputation, lest by any means I should run, or had run, in vain. (Galatians 2:2c) Paul didn't sneak in through the back door. False teachers usually sneak in among the people and start their trouble among the flock. **For there are certain men crept in unawares, who were before of old ordained to this condemnation, ungodly men, turning the grace of our God into lasciviousness, and denying the only Lord God, and our Lord Jesus Christ. (Jude 1:4)** The apostates and the Judaizers of Galatia had done just that. They crept in under the guise of being their friends but with the intention of destroying the gospel of grace and bringing the Galatian believers into bondage. Paul didn't sneak in like a wolf. The text says that he went in **privately to them which were of reputation.** That is he went straight to the Church leadership. They knew firsthand that Paul was there and what he was there for. Paul had instructed the Corinthians to, **Let all things be done decently and in order. (1 Corinthians 14:40)** This was the way Paul worked.

THE JUDAIZERS CONFRONTED

As we have just leaned, false teachers are devious and destructive. Paul points out that several false brethren had slipped into the Jerusalem Council. By calling them false brethren, Paul was saying that they were not true believers.

Paul's Dispute

But neither Titus, who was with me, being a Greek, was compelled to be circumcised: (Galatians 2:3) This was a bold move for Paul. This was an open confrontation of the legalist at the Jerusalem council. He had taken Titus with him for this very purpose. **And certain men which came down from Judaea taught the brethren, and said, Except ye be circumcised after the manner of Moses, ye cannot be saved. (Acts 15:1)** The Judaizers passionately pushed the rite of circumcision as necessary for salvation. However, Titus was a living example of someone who became a Christian without circumcision. The Jews required every convert to Judaism to be circumcised and they tried to carry their rules over into the Church and make it a requirement for getting saved. However, Titus wasn't becoming a Jew, he had become a Christian. Though Titus was a Christian and in the ministry with Paul, the Jerusalem Council did not require him to be circumcised. This proved to the Galatians that the leaders of the Jerusalem church were in agreement with the gospel of grace that Paul preached.

Paul's Discernment

And that because of false brethren unawares brought in, who came in privily to spy out our liberty which we have in Christ Jesus, that they might bring us into bondage: (Galatians 2:4) Here we see Paul's discernment is recognizing the presence and purpose of these underhanded Judaizers. From this verse we can learn three truths about these legalists.

First, **_their Depravity_**. By calling them **false brethren**, Paul was saying that they were not true believers. These were Jewish legalists. They were religious but lost.

Second, **_their Deceit_**. These were false brethren **unawares.** They had been successful at hiding their true identity. Like the apostates that Jude warned of, they had **crept in unawares. (Jude 1:4)** They had managed to stay under cover. Paul points out that they came in **privily.** They slipped in like wolves without the people knowing it. Paul says they snuck in to, ... **spy out our liberty which we have**

in Christ Jesus. They weren't there to learn. Their concern was not the truth, but the promotion of their own religion.

Third, ***their Desire***. Paul says, **...that they might bring us into bondage.** They had one major purpose for being there and that was to learn as much as possible so they could try to figure out a way to counter the gospel of God's grace. Their driving desire was to bring believers, who were set at liberty from the law through Christ, back under the bondage of the law.

Paul's Determination

To whom we gave place by subjection, no, not for an hour; that the truth of the gospel might continue with you. (Galatians 2:5) Paul was Relying on his Saviour, Resting in the Scriptures and Relentless in his Stand. Paul absolutely refused to yield to their doctrine even for the shortest amount of time. Giving them an opportunity to present their position would have given them a measure of credibility and to compromise the true gospel—it just could not be done. The word **subjection** means *"to yield, to give way, to retreat, or to retire."* When it came to defending the gospel Paul didn't have a compromising bone in his body.

THE JOINT CONCLUSION

But contrariwise, when they saw that the gospel of the uncircumcision was committed unto me, as the gospel of the circumcision was unto Peter; (For he that wrought effectually in Peter to the apostleship of the circumcision, the same was mighty in me toward the Gentiles:) (Galatians 2:7-8) The leaders of the Jerusalem church realized and agreed that Paul had been sent to the gentiles with equal authority and with the same message with which Peter had been sent to the Jews.

And when James, Cephas, and John, who seemed to be **pillars, perceived the grace that was given unto me, they gave to me and Barnabas the right hands of fellowship; that we should go unto the heathen, and they unto the circumcision. (Galatians 2:9)** The pillars of the Jerusalem Church gave Paul and Barnabas the **right hand of fellowship.** This was much more than the handshake that we are familiar with in the western word. It had a much greater significance in the ancient world. The **right hand of fellowship**. It signified a pledge of friendship and promise. The leaders of the Jerusalem Church were in full agreement with Paul and totally committed to the same gospel.

In Defense Of The Gospel
Galatians 2:11-21

It had been clearly determined at the Jerusalem Council that Gentiles were saved and added to the Church in the same way that the Jews were—through faith alone (Acts 15:7-9). However, it wasn't long before a new problem presented itself. The new issue was between the Jews who were still holding to the law concerning dietary regulations and the Gentiles who had no such custom. While it had been settled that Gentiles were now free to come into the church and fellowship with Jewish believers, the new issue was whether or not a Jew was free to enter into a Gentile home and eat Gentile foods. The issue soon erupted into quite a controversy with Peter caught in middle. Paul rebuking Peter at Antioch further proves the legitimacy of his apostleship. We will see that Paul's rebuke of Peter was based upon the solid foundation of doctrinal truth. In his argument and defense of the gospel of grace, Paul exposes the error and foolishness of going back to the law. The law condemns and brings death, not life. However, the gospel of grace is the way of life

PETER'S CAPITULATION

For before that certain came from James, he did eat with the Gentiles: but when they were come, he withdrew and separated himself, fearing them which were of the circumcision. (Galatians 2:12) As always there were folks on both sides and it is obvious that that issue had become quite divisive. Peter had gotten caught in middle and was a bit wish-washy capitulating between the two groups. Paul was no compromiser. He stepped in and set things in order.

It was Hurtful

For before that certain came from James, he did eat with the Gentiles: but when they were come, he withdrew and separated himself, fearing them which were of the circumcision. (Galatians 2:12) This issue resulted in an unnecessary division in the Church. The text says, **he did eat with the Gentiles.** That was the issue. Could a Jew eat Gentile food? At first Peter had no problem fellowshipping with the Gentiles. But when ... **certain came from James**, problems arose. Notice that they are described as **certain**. We can presume that these were men of position because of the effect they had on Peter when they showed up. They were the big shots from Jerusalem.

Peter **...withdrew and separated himself, fearing them which were of the circumcision.** Notice that they are identified as being **of the circumcision.** They were Jews and from the context we see which side of the issue they were on. Peter's reaction tells that these were men of power and reputation and he feared them.

When the big shots arrived Peter immediately **withdrew and separated himself** from the Gentile believers. And notice that Peter is described as **fearing them**. Peter was intimidated by their presence. Peter aligned with them because of who they were. He compromised principle for personality. The fear of man is an awful force. Solomon said, **The fear of man bringeth a snare: but whoso putteth his** trust in the LORD shall be safe. (Proverbs 29:25) The greatness of our fear usually shows the weakness of our faith. The fear of man is one of the greatest hindrances to serving God. It is described as a **snare**. A snare is an awful place. It is a place of **Detainment**. It grasps and holds its victims. It is a place of **Defeat** for the prey wears itself out trying to get free. Finally the snare becomes a place of **Death**. Fear cripples the work of God. **For God hath not given us the spirit of fear; but of power, and of love, and of a sound mind. (2 Timothy 1:7)**

It was Harmful

And the other Jews dissembled likewise with him; insomuch that Barnabas also was carried away with their dissimulation. (Galatians 2:13) Every Christian is a leader, at least to some degree. People are watching us and many of them will make decisions based on what they see in our lives. The Jews and even Barnabas followed Peter's lead. When we compromise, it influences others. Peter had learned earlier in his life that what he did influenced others.

> **There were together Simon Peter, and Thomas called Didymus, and Nathanael of Cana in Galilee, and the *sons* of Zebedee, and two other of his disciples. Simon Peter saith unto them, I go a fishing. They say unto him, We also go with thee. They went forth, and entered into a ship immediately; and that night they caught nothing. (John 21:2-3)**

Jesus had just been crucified. Peter had miserably failed his Lord. He was backslid and discouraged. The bottom had fallen out of Peter's life and he said, **I go a fishing.** Peter wasn't talking about getting his fishing pole and tackle box out and going down to the lake for a relaxing afternoon. Peter was actually quitting the ministry. He was forsaking his calling and going back to his old life. In his discouragement Peter was content to give up on God's call and fall back on his old trade of fishing. But notice that as soon as Peter said, **I go a fishing,** six others said, **We also go with thee.** Peter's decision not only affected himself, but everyone else that was standing there with him. The same is true of every believer. The decisions we make and the direction we take will influence others, either to the good or the bad. The same is true in our text. When Peter compromised, the Jews and Barnabas followed his lead.

It was Hypocrisy

Paul describes their actions as **...dissimulation. (Galatians 2:13b)** The word **dissimulation** is defined by Noah Webster as, *"The act of dissembling; a hiding under a false appearance; a feigning; false pretension; hypocrisy ... it includes also the assuming of a false or counterfeit appearance which conceals the real opinions or purpose."* The word was originally used to describe an actor, one who pretends to be someone or something he is not. The whole crowd, Peter, the Jews and Barnabas were hypocritical in their actions. They knew better, but unfortunately, they were motivated by personality rather than principle. They knew better, but they gave in to the pressure. Those who follow us need to see genuine Christianity. The best way to promote principle is to live it.

PAUL'S CORRECTION

Paul's confrontation with Peter was necessary in order to correct him. Not only had Peter's compromise caused unnecessary division among God's people, it was also contrary to the truth of the gospel.

Involved Personal Confrontation

But when Peter was come to Antioch, I withstood him to the face, because he was to be blamed. (Galatians 2:11) Notice first of all that Paul dealt with Peter to his face. He went straight to Peter. He didn't talk to others about Peter. Paul went directly to Peter to get this matter straightened out. The word **withstood** means *"to stand against, oppose, resist."* The word **blamed** means *"to censured, to disapprove, to find fault with."*

Involved Public Correction

But when I saw that they walked not uprightly according to the truth of the gospel, I said unto Peter before them all, If thou, being a Jew, livest after the manner of Gentiles, and not as do the Jews, why compellest thou the Gentiles to live as do the Jews? (Galatians 2:14) Now don't miss this. Notice that Paul states, **...I said unto Peter before them all.** Paul didn't just deal with the problem privately, he also addressed it publicly. Here is where a lot of Christians have difficulty dealing with correction. Public compromise many times calls for public correction. Don't misunderstand what is being said here. Certainly we don't advocate that every failure and every detail be dealt with publically. However, when the error is public in such a way that it influences others, there must be some degree of public correction. Paul dealt with Peter and then dealt with those who had been influenced by him. **Them that sin rebuke before all, that others also may fear. (1 Timothy 5:20)** We learn from other peoples correction. Solomon said, **Smite a scorner, and the simple will beware... (Proverbs 19:25)** The nature and influence of Peter sin required public correction.

Involved Principled Conviction

Knowing that a man is not justified by the works of the law, but by the faith of Jesus Christ, even we have believed in Jesus Christ, that we might be justified by the faith of Christ, and not by the works of the law: for by the works of the law shall no flesh be justified. (Galatians 2:16) Paul was acting on principle. He was earnestly contending for the for the faith. The previous verse points out that **the truth of the gospel** was at stake. Paul gets to the heart of the matter. How is a man justified before God? What they ate and who they ate with had no bearing on their salvation. Paul points out that **a man is not justified by the works of the law, but by the faith of Jesus Christ.** The word **justified** speaks of being declared righteous by God. We do not become righteous by keeping the law. We are warned that, **... by the works of the law shall no flesh be justified.** Paul said, **Therefore by the deeds of the law there shall no flesh be justified in his sight: for by the law is the knowledge of sin. (Romans 3:20)**

Our salvation and standing before God is not due to any merit of our own. It is not because we have met and satisfied the righteous demands of the law. Such an achievement is humanly impossible. Paul is pointing out that ritual does not result in righteousness. Justification is through faith in Jesus Christ.

But if, while we seek to be justified by Christ, we ourselves also are found sinners, is therefore Christ the minister of sin? God forbid. (Galatians 2:17) Paul offers an argument based on the claims of Christ. Jesus Christ promised to save all who would come to Him and receive Him as Saviour. **But as many as received him, to them gave he power to become the sons of God, even to them that believe on his name: (John 1:12)** Not only did Jesus Christ claim to be the way to Heave, He also claimed to be the only way. **Jesus saith unto him, I am the way, the truth, and the life: no man cometh unto the Father, but by me. (John 14:6)** Here is Paul's argument. If receiving Christ fails to justify one before God then the promises and claims of Christ were lies and He was a fraud. If we must keep any law or observe any ritual in order to be saved then there is only one conclusion—Christ would be the minister of sin. Paul says, **God forbid.**

For if I build again the things which I destroyed, I make myself a transgressor. (Galatians 2:18) The word **destroyed** means to *"tear down, dissolve, bring to nought."* Paul had once trusted in the law to justify him before God. However, on the Damascus road he realized under the mighty hand of God that the law he loved and contended for was not the way to Heaven. Paul was saved by the grace of God and went on under the direction of God to preach the message of grace to the Gentiles. When Paul put his trust in Christ the law was destroyed so far as justification was concerned. To go back to a system that he had destroyed and try to build again upon it would make him a transgressor. To observe Jewish ritual after being saved is inconsistent with the message of grace that God had entrusted to him.

Crucified With Christ
Galatians 2:19-21

Paul now draws a practical conclusion and deals with the fact that the believer is dead to the law. Anyone who lives under the law, lives under the condemnation of death. However, in Christ the law has been satisfied by our Saviour. Therefore, we are dead to the law and raise in newness of life.

A PUNITIVE CONDEMNATION

For I through the law am dead to the law, that I might live unto God. (Galatians 2:19) Although one cannot be saved by keeping the law, it does, nevertheless play an important role in bring the sinner to Christ. Paul said, **But we know that the law is good, if a man use it lawfully; (1 Timothy 1:8)** Paul was brought up under the law and had tried to satisfy its demands of righteousness. Though he had excelled at it he still came up short (Philippians 3:4-9). It always comes down to man's righteousness verses Christ's righteousness.

When Paul said, **I through the law am dead to the law**, he was saying that the law had passed the death sentence upon Him. Paul dealt with this in the book of Romans.

> **But sin, taking occasion by the commandment, wrought in me all manner of concupiscence. For without the law sin *was* dead. For I was alive without the law once: but when the commandment came, sin revived, and I died. And the commandment, which *was ordained* to life, I**

found *to be* unto death. For sin, taking occasion by the commandment, deceived me, and by it slew *me*. Wherefore the law *is* holy, and the commandment holy, and just, and good. Was then that which is good made death unto me? God forbid. But sin, that it might appear sin, working death in me by that which is good; that sin by the commandment might become exceeding sinful. (Romans 7:8-13)

When a man attempts to live by the law, it always results in death. The law had killed Paul in the sense that it found him guilty and produced the sentence upon him. Paul had broken the law and therefore he stood guilty before God. This is the purpose of the law. The law shows us that we cannot become good enough to get to Heaven by keeping it. **For whosoever shall keep the whole law, and yet offend in one point, he is guilty of all. (James 2:10)** No matter how hard we try or even how far we get, we still come up short. God never intended that the law save us, but rather to show us that we need Christ. **Wherefore the law was our schoolmaster to bring us unto Christ, that we might be justified by faith. But after that faith is come, we are no longer under a schoolmaster. (Galatians 3:24-25)** The law was designed to teach man his sinfulness and inadequacy to satisfy a Holy God. Thus, causing him to trust in Christ and be justified by faith.

A PERSONAL CRUCIFIXION

I am crucified with Christ... (Galatians 2:20a) When Jesus Christ died on the cross the believer was spiritually crucified with Him. So far as our position goes, we died with Christ, rose with Him, ascended with Him, and are seated with Him in Heaven.

> **Know ye not, that so many of us as were baptized into Jesus Christ were baptized into his death? Therefore we are buried with him by baptism into death: that like as Christ was raised up from the dead by the glory of the Father, even so we also should walk in newness of life. For if we have been planted together in the likeness of his death, we shall be also *in the likeness* of *his* resurrection: Knowing this, that our old man is crucified with *him*, that the body of sin might be destroyed, that henceforth we should not serve sin. (Romans 6:3-6)**

> **And you *hath he quickened*, who were dead in trespasses and sins; Wherein in time past ye walked according to the course of this world, according to the prince of the power of the air, the spirit that now worketh in the children of disobedience: Among whom also we all had our conversation in times past in the lusts of our flesh, fulfilling the desires of the flesh and of the mind; and were by nature the children of wrath, even as others. But God, who is rich in mercy, for his great love wherewith he loved us, Even when we were dead in sins, hath quickened us together with Christ, (by grace ye are saved;) And hath raised *us* up together, and made *us* sit together in heavenly *places* in Christ Jesus: (Ephesians 2:1-6)**

In Christ the believer is dead to the penalty of the law because Jesus bore the wrath of God as his substitute. Because we are in Christ we are dead to the law and the flesh.

In these passages the Bible speaks of a specific act of Almighty God in every believer when he comes to Christ as his Saviour. As far as God is concerned every believer's old nature is dead and nailed to the cross.

There is also a part that is the believer's responsibility. **And they that are Christ's have crucified the flesh with the affections and lusts. (Galatians 5:24)** We see here that it is the believer himself that does the crucifying. We are to die to sin and be alive to righteousness. **Likewise reckon ye also yourselves to be dead indeed unto sin, but alive unto God through Jesus Christ our Lord. (Romans 6:12)** God has declared the believer dead in Christ. Now it is our responsibility to **reckon** our own selves dead. It is not enough to be declared crucified and dead. We must by faith reckon it to be true in our own life. The word **reckon** means *"to count, to number, to calculate."* It is a bookkeeping term. The idea is that of reconciling a checkbook. We take the bank statement and our checkbook, sit down and make the checkbook agree with the bank statement. That is what God is saying when He commands that we *reckon* ourselves to be dead. God has already declared it to be so. The only thing left is for us to bring our life in line with His word. Reckoning is the step of faith that acknowledges what God says about me in the Bible is now true in my life.

A PARADOX CONFIRMED

Paul said, **...nevertheless I live; (Galatians 2:20b)** This is indeed a paradox! Crucifixion results in death! Paul has been crucified, yet he is living. How can that be? The answer is simple! Paul was now living the resurrected life. The old man had been rendered powerless and Paul was now walking in newness of life. Real life starts when we are saved. **For sin shall not have dominion over you: for ye are not under the law, but under grace. (Romans 6:14)** Since we are no longer slaves to sin we can walk a new course in life.

A PRESENT COMPANION

Paul says, yet not I, but Christ liveth in me: the life which I now live in the flesh I live by the faith of the Son of God, (Galatians 2:20c) This new life is the result of the resurrection of Jesus Christ. It is not because we have been able to keep the law and overcome death. It is all because Christ died and rose again. It is entirely by His and not our works. Think carefully about these words. Paul said, **Christ liveth in me.** Just before Jesus was crucified He told His disciples, **Yet a little while, and the world seeth me no more; but ye see me: because I live, ye shall live also. At that day ye shall know that I am in my Father, and ye in me, and I in you. (John 14:19-20)** Every believer can say, **Christ liveth in me.** The Bible declares, **Christ in you, the hope of glory: (Colossians 1:27)**

A PRACTICAL CONCLUSION

I do not frustrate the grace of God: for if righteousness come by the law, then Christ is dead in vain. (Galatians 2:21) The word **frustrate** is from the Greek *"atheteo"* and means *"to set aside, nullify it, or make it void."* Any trust in religious rituals or good works for salvation nullifies the grace God. Therefore, to trust in any form of religious works is to nullify grace. It frustrates the grace of God because if a man could earn salvation, then God must give him what he deserves. However, the very nature of grace is that God gives us what we do not deserve.

Paul said, **if righteousness come by the law, then Christ is dead in vain.** The word **vain** means *"without a cause, rendered useless."* Paul told the Romans, **Now to him that worketh is the reward not reckoned of grace, but of debt. (Romans 4:4)** A works salvation nullifies the grace principle and renders Christ's death on the cross useless and empty because if we can get to Heaven by good works then God would not have to have given His Son for us.

Bewitched
Galatians 3:1-5

In Chapter 3, we come to the second division of the letter where he deals with grace and the law. Paul shows that grace has always been God's design for the salvation of man and at the same time corrects the lie that salvation by grace was a new and erroneous doctrine.

THE ERROR OF THEIR DOCTRINE

O foolish Galatians, who hath bewitched you, that ye should not obey the truth, before whose eyes Jesus Christ hath been evidently set forth, crucified among you? (Galatians 3:1) We don't have to be worried about Paul beating around the bush. He takes the bull by the horns and gets right to the heart of the matter.

They were Deficient in their Discernment

O foolish Galatians... (Galatians 3:1a) Paul uses this word twice in this short section of five verses. Paul's words no doubt cut straight to the heart of those who had accepted the false teaching of the Judaizers. The word **foolish** comes from *"anoetos"* and carries the idea of *"ignorant, no understanding, unwise."* It speaks of someone who lacks spiritual insight or discernment. They had been taught the truth. But they had been foolish in that they failed in testing the Judaizers against the truth they had been taught. As a result, the Judaizers led them away from the truth and into bondage. This was indeed a sharp rebuke, but it was a biblical rebuke. Paul told Titus concerning deceivers, **Wherefore rebuke them sharply, that they may be sound in the faith; (Titus 1:13)** The word **sharply** means *"severely, abruptly, curtly, in a manner that cuts, rudely."* It means that we are not to beat around the bush and mince words about it. The reason for such sharp rebuke is **that they may be sound in the faith.**

They were Deep in their Deception

Paul asks **who hath bewitched you? (Galatians 3:1b)** The word **bewitched** comes from *"baskaino"* and means *"to charm or fascinate by false representation."* It carries the idea of bringing evil upon someone by using flattery and false praise. The legalists had charmed the Galatians into their legalism. The false teachers had presented themselves and their devilish doctrine along with their flattery of the Galatians in such a way that that the Galatians were mesmerized and captivated as if they were under a spell. The Galatians had fallen for the oldest trick in the book. In their lack of discernment they had fallen under the charm of flattery.

> **A man that flattereth his neighbour spreadeth a net for his feet. (Proverbs 29:5)**

Flattery is defined as *"False praise; commendation bestowed for the purpose of gaining favor and influence..."* (Webster) Man loves to be praised and the Bible does teaches us to give honor to whom it is due (Romans 13:7). But the lust for praise gives the devil every opportunity to lay his net at our feet. There is a serious warning here for every believer. If we are not careful we can get just as sidetracked as the Galatians did. We are warned many times.

> **Lest Satan should get an advantage of us: for we are not ignorant of his devices. (2 Corinthians 2:11)**

> **But I fear, lest by any means, as the serpent beguiled Eve through his subtilty, so your minds should be corrupted from the simplicity that is in Christ. (2 Corinthians 11:3)**

We are commanded to, **Put on the whole armour of God, that ye may be able to stand against the wiles of the devil. (Ephesians 6:11)** The word **wiles** comes from *"methodeias"* from which the word *"method"* is derived. Satan has his methods of attack. Satan is a ruthless and merciless enemy who will stop at nothing in trying to defeat God's people. One of his methods is the use of false teachers like the Judaizers who captivated the hearts of the Galatians. Satan can present himself and his false teachers in such a way as to mesmerize and charm even the people of God. Paul warned of his abilities when he wrote of the false apostles of Corinth. **For such are false apostles, deceitful workers, transforming themselves into the apostles of Christ. And no marvel; for Satan himself is transformed into an angel of light. (2 Corinthians 11:13-14)** The foolish Galatians had been duped and brought into the bondage of legalism by these deceitful workers. However, God's desire for us is **That we henceforth be no more children, tossed to and fro, and carried about with every wind of doctrine, by the sleight of men, and cunning craftiness, whereby they lie in wait to deceive; (Ephesians 4:14)** The word **sleight** is a gambling term and speaks of trickery and fraud. The word **craftiness** is used in the Bible to describe the way the Pharisees dealt with Jesus. It is also used of the serpent deceiving of Eve. These speak of deceivers who speak cunningly and shrewdly. They sound correct and they are convincing, but they are wrong and dangerous.

They were Disobedient in their Doctrine

...that ye should not obey the truth, before whose eyes Jesus Christ hath been evidently set forth, crucified among you? (Galatians 3:1c) The words **evidently set forth** comes from *"prografo"* and means *"to write before."* The idea is that of posting a public notice. It was used of posters, signs or public announcements that were placed out in the streets where the general public could see them. That is what Paul had done with the gospel. He had so clearly preached and presented the truth of salvation by grace that they were without excuse not to understand. Both the details and the implications of the crucifixion were very clearly presented.

Notice that they had **not obeyed the truth.** This was their biggest problem. They knew the truth but they didn't obey it. They were spellbound by the ear tickling and platitudes of the Judaizers. They were in trouble because they didn't take the truth seriously. They were without excuse. They knew the trust, but failed to keep it. Jesus said, **...If ye continue in my word, then are ye my disciples indeed; And ye shall know the truth, and the truth shall make you free. (John 8:31-32)** The Galatians had failed to continue in the word and as a result had become **entangled again with the yoke of bondage. (Galatians 5:1)** They were no longer disciples of Christ. They were actually disciples of the satanic Judaizers.

Paul hit their error head on and now he proceeds by asking four questions concerning the Spirit, their Sanctification and suffering. The questions are designed to prove that works and law have no part in attaining that which God has freely given.

THE EVIDENCE OF THEIR DEPARTURE

This only would I learn of you, Received ye the Spirit by the works of the law, or by the hearing of faith? (Galatians 3:2) Paul starts this question with the statement, **This only would I learn of you...** This wasn't an offer to concede if the Galatians could present an argument for their position. He wasn't saying, *"Explain yourself, maybe you can convince me."* Paul knew where he stood and he was grounded in the truth. Paul was drawing the Galatians into a dialogue. He then presented them with four questions that disarmed them and left them defenseless in their foolishness.

Paul asks, ... **Received ye the Spirit by the works of the law, or by the hearing of faith? (Galatians 3:2)** There is only one possible answer to this question. The Holy Spirit indwells the believer at the moment of salvation. Paul said, **... if any man have not the Spirit of Christ, he is none of his. (Romans 8:9)** The Spirit is never received by works but by faith. The Holy Spirit comes to indwell the life of new believers the very moment they receive Jesus Christ as Saviour. **Jesus answered, Verily, verily, I say unto thee, Except a man be born of water and of the Spirit, he cannot enter into the kingdom of God. That which is born of the flesh is flesh; and that which is born of the Spirit is spirit.**

(John 3:5-6) This is the regenerating work of the Holy Spirit. **Not by works of righteousness which we have done, but according to his mercy he saved us, by the washing of regeneration, and renewing of the Holy Ghost. (Titus 3:5)** Noah Webster defines **regeneration** as *"Reproduction; the act of producing anew."* Our first birth was the result of a regeneration from our parents. The second birth is also a regeneration. It is a spiritual birth from the Holy Spirit as He imparts to us new spiritual life. Every born again believer has the Spirit of God permanently living in his life. The answer to Paul's question is obvious. Of course, the Holy Spirit is received by faith, not by the works of the law.

THE EXAMPLE OF THEIR DEFEAT

Are ye so foolish? having begun in the Spirit, are ye now made perfect by the flesh? (Galatians 3:3) Again, the **flesh** speaks of the natural man as he is without out Christ. The lost man does not have the Holy Spirit. Everything he does is accomplished with the power of his own ability and no lasting good comes of it. Jesus said, **the flesh profiteth nothing. (John 6:63)** The Galatians had been saved by the grace of God. However, they were being taught to return to the law to receive God's favor and maintain their Christian life. What they had started by grace they were attempting to finish by works. Grace is God doing for us what we cannot do for ourselves, Works is man's attempt to reach and satisfy God in one's own power.

Paul asks, **are ye now made perfect by the flesh?** The word **perfect** is from the Greek *"epiteleo."* It carries the idea of *"bringing something to completion."* They had been saved by the regenerating work of the Spirit, but it didn't stop there. The Spirit of God continues in the believer's life to perfect him, that is, to bring his salvation to completion. Paul had taught the Philippian believers the same truth. **Being confident of this very thing, that he which hath begun a good work in you will perform it until the day of Jesus Christ: (Philippians 1:6)** The word **perform** in this verse is the Greek word (*epiteleo*) for **perfect** in our text verse. The work of the Holy Spirit begins with bringing a person to salvation, then He continues to conform the believer to the image of Christ.

Paul had referred to them as **foolish Galatians**. It is absolutely foolish for one to think that anything spiritual can be achieved through the power of the flesh. If a believer's new life in Christ began with a supernatural work of the Holy Spirit, it must continue in the same.

THE EMPTINESS OF THEIR DISTRESS

Have ye suffered so many things in vain? if it be yet in vain. (Galatians 3:4) The Galatians had embraced the Christian faith and they had been persecuted for it. In the early days of Christianity those who converted to Christ were made to suffer for their faith. The Jews were relentless in persecuting the early Church. The Galatians had been on the receiving end of the persecution. The suffering referred to here is found in Acts 14:2-22. After his first missionary journey Paul along with Barnabas had gone back and ministered to the Galatian converts during their time of great suffering and persecution.

> **And when they had preached the gospel to that city, and had taught many, they returned again to Lystra, and to Iconium, and Antioch, Confirming**

the souls of the disciples, and exhorting them to continue in the faith, and that we must through much tribulation enter into the kingdom of God. (Acts 14:21-22)

The message that had stirred up so much anger and resulted in so much persecution was the message of justification by faith through Jesus Christ alone. **Be it known unto you therefore, men and brethren, that through this man is preached unto you the forgiveness of sins: And by him all that believe are justified from all things, from which ye could not be justified by the law of Moses. (Acts 13:38-39)** The Galatian believers who once stood so strong and suffered for the truth had been duped into reverting back to the law. Paul asks the question, **Have ye suffered so many things in vain?** Paul is saying, "if the Judaizers are right in their doctrine, then you were fools for suffering for Christ as you did."

THE EXTENT OF THEIR DECEPTION

He therefore that ministereth to you the Spirit, and worketh miracles among you, doeth he it by the works of the law, or by the hearing of faith? (Galatians 3:5) God had given the Galatian believers the Holy Spirit and He had worked miracles among them. Paul's question is, did God do this **by the works of the law, or by the hearing of faith?** No one could doubt the fact of these great things had been accomplished as a result of God's grace.

Abraham And The Gospel
Galatians 3:6-18

Now Paul brings Abraham into the argument. In fact Paul will refer to Abraham eight times in this chapter (3:6, 7, 8, 9, 14, 16, 18, 29). Abraham was the physical father of the Jewish race. He was highly respected and revered by the Jews and would carry a lot of weight in Paul's argument.

THE FAITH OF ABRAHAM

The Juziazers and the Galatians had missed the truth that Abraham had been justified by faith and not by works. Paul's argument is that since Abraham was the first Jew and God justified him by faith, God unquestionably will justify his followers by faith also. Paul presents five facts about Abraham's faith.

The Practice Of Abraham's Faith

Even as Abraham believed God ... (Galatians 3:6a) Paul drives his point home with a direct quote from the Old Testament (Genesis 15:6). This is a passage that the Juziazers and the Galatians would have been familiar with. The word **even** here is important. It comes from the Greek *"kathos"* and means *"even as, according as, as well as."* The idea that Paul is presenting here is that all people are saved the same way Abraham was saved. Abraham's salvation is the pattern of salvation for all people throughout all ages. That doesn't mean that God saves people in different ways. Everyone who ever was saved or ever will be saved is saved by the same principal as Abraham was saved.

> **Now the LORD had said unto Abram, Get thee out of thy country, and from thy kindred, and from thy father's house, unto a land that I will shew thee: And I will make of thee a great nation, and I will bless thee, and make thy name great; and thou shalt be a blessing: And I will bless them that bless thee, and curse him that curseth thee: and in thee shall all families of the earth be blessed. (Genesis 12:1-3)**

This was a big order for Abraham. He was to leave everything and set out as a pilgrim. He wasn't even told where he was going. Leaving Ur meant that Abraham was to abandon his roots, sever all ties, leave the comforts of home and set out on a journey to a place that only God knew. But all of that was ok with Abraham because God was everything to him.

Now notice that the text says, **Abraham believed God...** True faith is believing God. It is important to take note that the basis of Abraham's faith was not the promise, but the God of the promise. Too often folks talk about what they believe rather than Who they believe. Oh Abraham believed in the promise and he fully expected everything that God promised him. However, Abraham's basis for expecting the promise was his faith in the God who promised. Abraham had a spiritual mindset. His focus was on the eternal rather than the temporal. What God promised Abraham was far more than a piece of land and an extended family. Abraham understood that the land of Canaan was not the fulfillment of God's promise.

> **By faith Abraham, when he was called to go out into a place which he should after receive for an**

> inheritance, obeyed; and he went out, not knowing whither he went. By faith he sojourned in the land of promise, as *in* a strange country, dwelling in tabernacles with Isaac and Jacob, the heirs with him of the same promise: For he looked for a city which hath foundations, whose builder and maker *is* God. (Hebrews 11:8-10)

Abraham lived in the land of Canaan, but he never settled down there. He **sojourned in the land of promise, as in a strange country, dwelling in tabernacles.** He knew that Canaan was not his true home. He considered himself a pilgrim there. He never built a house but rather lived in tents. The word **sojourned** comes from the Greek *"paroikeo"* and means *"to reside as a foreigner, to be a stranger."* Abraham spent his life in a tent because he knew that what he was looking for was not to be found in this world. **For he looked for a city which hath foundations, whose builder and maker is God. (Hebrews 8:10)** The point is that his faith in God kept him looking for what God had promised. What faith!

The Pleasing Of Abraham's Faith

Paul declares that Abraham's faith **... was as accounted to him for righteousness. (Galatians 3:6b) For what saith the scripture? Abraham believed God, and it was counted unto him for righteousness. (Romans 4:3)** This Scripture clearly teaches that Abraham was justified by faith. **He believed God** and that is how he was justified. Faith is the vehicle by which we are saved. The word **accounted** comes from *"logizomai"* and means *"to count, impute, reckon."* It is a word that comes from the business and legal world that carries the idea of *"crediting to an account."* It would be like going to the bank and depositing $1000.00. The bank applies that money to your account. So Abraham believed God, and God in effect got out His book and put it down to Abraham's account as righteousness. This is imputed righteousness. When we believe God and by faith trust in Christ, God takes out the book and credits Christ's righteousness to our account. **For he hath made him to be sin for us, who knew no sin; that we might be made the righteousness of God in him (2 Corinthians 5:21)** That is how He saved Abraham and that is how He saves today.

The Posterity Of Abraham's Faith

Know ye therefore that they which are of faith, the same are the children of Abraham. (Galatians 3:7) The Jews prided themselves in being the children of Abraham. The Jews caustically ask Christ, **Art thou greater than our father Abraham, which is dead? and the prophets are dead: whom makest thou thyself? (John 8:53)** Think about it. There stood the Messiah in their midst. He was trying to reach them with the truth and they were holding on to their tradition. The Jews loved to identify themselves with Abraham. Paul says, **they which are of faith, the same are the children of Abraham.** If you are going to be a son of Abraham you with must be justified before God the same way that Abraham was. Salvation is a matter of faith. Those who come to God by faith in Christ are Abraham's decedents.

And the scripture, foreseeing that God would justify the heathen through faith, preached before the gospel unto Abraham, saying, In thee shall all nations be blessed. (Galatians 3:7-8) In His dealings with Abraham God foresaw the salvation of the Gentile nations. Abrahams faith and relationship with God was an illustration or a type of New Testament salvation. How the hyper-dispensationalists read the Bible and come up with a half a dozen or so plans of salvation is beyond me.

THE FACT OF THE LAW

Paul moves on to the law itself pointing out the impossibility of sinful man to satisfy the standards of the law and the consequences for attempting to get to God by way of the law.

The Letter Of The Law

For as many as are of the works of the law are under the curse: for it is written, Cursed is every one that continueth not in all things which are written in the book of the law to do them. (Galatians 3:10) No one except Jesus Christ has ever kept the law. He obeyed to the letter and perfectly fulfilled the law (Matthew 5:17). However, we cannot do that. Not only have we violated the law we are habitual offenders. We have broken the law over and over. Paul points out that no one can get to Heaven by obeying the law because no one is capable of full obedience to the law. **Cursed is every one that continueth not in all things which are written in the book of the law to do them.** Dealing with the same issue James said, **For whosoever shall keep the whole law, and yet offend in one point, he is guilty of all. (James 2:10)** The laws standard is perfect obedience all the time. It is perfect obedience **in all things which are written in the book of the law.** This isn't just the ten commandments. No man can keep and perfectly obey just the ten commandments, let alone the whole law of God. Yet the letter of the law requires continual and perfect obedience. That means every law of God along with the ceremonies, sacrifices and Holy days right down to the letter. All it takes is one infraction. Just one simple violation results in a person being a lawbreaker. Just one lie, one act of fornication, one adulterous fling. Stealing one small item. Taking the Lord's name in vain just once. It matters not what the sin is, how great or how small, if any part of the law is violated, the whole is violated. It is the breaking of God's law and renders the offender a criminal and guilty before God. Paul says that the one who is guilty of breaking the law is **cursed.** The word cursed comes from the Greek *"epikataratos"* and means *"to be cursed by God and doomed to punishment."* The law cannot save, it can only render one guilty and condemned. Such is the present condition of all who do not know Christ as Saviour.

The Limitation Of The Law

But that no man is justified by the law in the sight of God, it is evident: for, The just shall live by faith. (Galatians 3:11) Here is a dogmatic declaration from the inspired writer. Here the whole matter is summed up. Paul said, **no man is justified by the law in the sight of God.** Folks say, "I know I'm not perfect and I've made mistakes, but I'm not a bad person. As long as my good outweighs my bad I'll go to Heaven." No! You're wrong. Jesus died to pay man's sin debt and apart from a personal relationship with Him you are guilty and condemned already and on your way to the lake of fire for all eternity. Jesus said, **He that believeth on him is not condemned: but he that believeth not is condemned already, because he hath not believed in the name of the only begotten Son of God. (John 3:18)**

Jesus perfectly obeyed the law and died for sinners. It is only by His finished work on the cross that man can be justified.

The just shall live by faith. This truth is stated three other times in God's word (Habakkuk 2:4, Romans 1:17, Hebrews 10:38) It is not our works but our faith that pleases God. **But without faith it is impossible to please him: for he that cometh to God must believe that he is, and that he is a rewarder of them that diligently seek him. (Hebrews 11:6)** God rewards man on the basis of his faith. That is how he saved Abraham and that is how He saves us. Paul said, **And the law is not of faith: but, The man that doeth them shall live in them. (Galatians 3:12)** The man who attempts to keep the law is not trusting God, rather his own ability. However, man of faith trusts God to justify him. Paul said, **The man that doeth them shall live in them.** Anyone who is attempting to live under the law is living under a curse. A man will live and die under the curse of the law except he come to God by faith in Jesus Christ. **The just shall live by faith.**

THE FREEDOM IN CHRIST

Paul goes on to explain that Christ paid the full penalty of the law for the sinner. He fully satisfied the righteous demands of the law and as our sacrifice took upon Himself our punishment.

The Saviour's Purchase

Christ hath redeemed us from the curse of the law, being made a curse for us: for it is written, Cursed is every one

that hangeth on a tree: (Galatians 3:13) The word **redeemed** is a familiar one. It comes from *"exagorazo"* and means *"to buy or rescue."* It carries the idea of paying a satisfactory price for a person or thing. The word was used in Bible times of purchasing a slave from the auction block. That slave was in bondage. He had nothing. He could not purchase his own freedom. He was bound to whoever paid the price for him. That is a picture of all of us. Mankind is bound by sin and can do nothing to freed himself. He is a slave and cannot make a satisfactory payment for his sin. Therefore, Christ was **made a curse for us.** The curse was upon us all for **all have sinned and come short of the glory of God. (Romans 3:23)** But Jesus stepped in and took the curse upon Himself. Christ paid the redemptive price and redeemed us. The purchase price was His blood. **Forasmuch as ye know that ye were not redeemed with corruptible things, as silver and gold, from your vain conversation received by tradition from your fathers; But with the precious blood of Christ, as of a lamb without blemish and without spot. (1 Peter 1:18-19)** That is why the text declares that **Christ hath redeemed us.** Not the law. Not our good works. Not our baptism, church membership, not even our religion, but Jesus Christ.

The Spirit's Power

That the blessing of Abraham might come on the Gentiles through Jesus Christ; that we might receive the promise of the Spirit through faith. (Galatians 3:14) It is interesting that in the context of law and faith Paul gets into the doctrine of the Holy Spirit. It is by His power that we live the Christian life. **Not by might, nor by power, but by my spirit, saith the LORD of hosts. (Zechariah 4:6)**

THE FIDELITY OF THE COVENANT

Brethren, I speak after the manner of men; Though it be but a man's covenant, yet if it be confirmed, no man disannulleth, or addeth thereto. (Galatians 3:15) Paul draws an analogy from the business world. A **covenant** it is a contract between two parties. It sets forth an agreement between the parties involved with terms and conditions. Once it has been agreed upon and signed, then the contract becomes legally binding. Neither party has the right to change the contract. Paul goes on to point out that in the same way, the contract between God and Abraham was confirmed and cannot be set aside or changed.

Now to Abraham and his seed were the promises made. He saith not, And to seeds, as of many; but as of one, And to thy seed, which is Christ. (Galatians 3:16) Paul refers to God's promise to Abraham. **And in thy seed shall all the nations of the earth be blessed; because thou hast obeyed my voice. (Genesis 22:18)** The word seed refers to the many descendants of Abraham beginning with Isaac. However, Paul narrows the meaning down to one person—Jesus Christ. Christ is the Son of Abraham (Matthew 1:1) and therefore the rightful heir to the covenant promise. Through Him the law and the promises of God were fulfilled. It is through Christ that we are saved.

And this I say, that the covenant, that was confirmed before of God in Christ, the law, which was four hundred and thirty years after, cannot disannul, that it should make the promise of none effect. (Galatians 3:17) It was 430 years after God's promise to Abraham that He gave the law to Moses. Paul argues that the law did not change or make void in any way God's Covenant with Abraham. The law could not and did not change God's covenant with Abraham. God gave Abraham His word and that is unchangeable. **In hope of eternal life, which God, that cannot lie, promised before the world began; (Titus 1:2)**

For if the inheritance be of the law, it is no more of promise: but God gave it to Abraham by promise. (Galatians 3:18) The **inheritance** refers to the promised blessings of the Abrahamic Covenant that in him all the nations of the earth would be blessed. If the promise had been conditional on keeping the law, then it would no longer be a promise. Keeping the law requires man's effort. If he does well he has earned the reward. However, God's promise to Abraham was given on the basis of grace alone. Paul's argument is that if there is any mixture of law and grace or faith and works, then it is no more of grace.

God's Schoolmaster
Galatians 3:19-29

After offering several arguments proving that salvation cannot be attained by the law, Paul goes on to explain the purpose of the law. Over 3000 years ago the law was given to Moses by God upon Mount Sinai. These commandants provide the structure for a moral lifestyle and society. These laws establish boundaries and clearly define the limits within which man is to live as commanded by God. These great commandments teach us of our inability to perfectly obey God, that we are sinners, and unable to please God in the power of our flesh, thereby, bringing us to a saving knowledge and faith in Jesus Christ.

THE PURPOSE OF THE LAW

Wherefore then serveth the law? It was added because of transgressions, till the seed should come to whom the promise was made; and it was ordained by angels in the hand of a mediator. Now a mediator is not a mediator of one, but God is one. (Galatians 3:19-20) The Judaizers might come back with the question, **Wherefore then serveth the law?** If salvation has always been by grace through faith and the Abrahamic promise was fulfilled in Christ, what was the purpose of the law to start with? Sometimes believers have the tendency to ignore the law as something that is done and over with. We often hear folks proclaim, *"We are not under the law, but under grace."* I do understand that we are not bound to ceremonial law.

However, the morel law of God is absolute for all ages and all people. Even as New Testament Christians we need to understand that the law is not something to be detested, but something to delight in.

> **But his delight is in the law of the Lord; and in his law doth he meditate day and night. (Psalms 1:2)**
>
> **O how love I thy law! it is my meditation all the day. (Psalms 119:97)**
>
> **Great peace have they which love thy law: and nothing shall offend them. (Psalms 119:165)**
>
> **But we know that the law is good, if a man use it lawfully; Knowing this, that the law is not made for a righteous man, but for the lawless and disobedient, for the ungodly and for sinners, for unholy and profane, for murderers of fathers and murderers of mothers, for manslayers, For whoremongers, for them that defile themselves with mankind, for menstealers, for liars, for perjured persons, and if there be any other thing that is contrary to sound doctrine; (1 Timothy 1:8-10)**

Wherefore then serveth the law? Paul answers, **It was added because of transgressions.** It is through the law that the awareness of sin comes. The law was given to show men that they are hopelessly sinful and in need of God's help. Paul said to the Roman believers, **I had not known sin, but by the law: for I had not known lust, except the law had said, Thou shalt not covet. (Romans 7:7b)** Paul is saying, I wouldn't have known what sin was if the law hadn't revealed it to me. **But sin, taking occasion by the commandment, wrought in me all manner of concupiscence. For without the law sin was dead. (Romans 7:8) Concupiscence** is *"a lust for that which is carnal and unlawful."* Paul knew what lust was and that it is sinful because the law said, **Thou shalt not covet.** The idea here is that the law exposed his sin of lust. **Moreover the law entered, that the offence might abound... (Romans 5:20a)** We could never understand what sin is unless we have some standard to judge by. The law is that standard. Without the law there is no sin. Without God's commandments there can be no transgression. James speaks of the law as a mirror that reflects man's sinful condition (James 1:23-24). The law is God's standard of righteousness that enables us to distinguish between good and evil. Therefore, the law shows man what he is—a sinner!

THE PROGRAM OF THE LAW

Is the law then against the promises of God? God forbid: for if there had been a law given which could have given life, verily righteousness should have been by the law. (Galatians 3:21) Paul deals with another objection that might be raised by the Judaizers. If what Paul has been saying is true, doesn't that mean that the law and grace contradict one another? Paul answers, **God forbid...** The phrase **God forbid** is the strongest negative Greek expression and carries the idea of *"an absolute impossibility."* The idea is perish the thought! There is no basis whatsoever for such foolish thinking.

... for if there had been a law given which could have given life, verily righteousness should have been by the

law. Paul stresses the fact that the law was never intended to give life. If a man could have perfectly obeyed and kept the law, he could have been saved on the basis of perfect obedience to the law. However, no man can perfectly keep the law. To transgress on one point is to be guilty of the whole. James said, **For whosoever shall keep the whole law, and yet offend in one point, he is guilty of all. (James 2:10)** The law demands perfect righteousness and therefore cannot result in eternal life. There is nothing wrong with the law. The problem is with man. He can't obey it.

THE PARAMETER OF THE LAW

But the scripture hath concluded all under sin... (Galatians 3:22a) The word **concluded** comes from the Greek *"synkleio"* and means *"to shut together, to include, to enclose, to shut up."* The idea is that of being shut up and hemmed in on all sides. Paul used a similar expression in Romans.

> **But now we are delivered from the law, that being dead wherein we were held; that we should serve in newness of spirit, and not in the oldness of the letter. (Romans 7:6)**

Paul says, **But now,** that is now that we are saved, we have been **delivered from the law, that being dead wherein we were held.** The word **held** speaks of being *"seized or retained"* That was our relationship to the law. We were hopelessly held as a prisoner. No matter how hard we tried to obtain righteousness, the flesh kept driving us to sin and the law continued to condemn. The law could not set us free. It could only show us our sinfulness, pronounce us guilty and condemn us to death.

Apart from Christ everyone is in the same fix. **All** are sinners. The sinner is hemmed in by his sin and on top of that the law has pronounced him guilty and holds him as a prisoner. There are no exceptions. **There is none righteous, no, not one: (Romans 3:10)** No man has ever satisfied the righteous demands of the law. We can attempt, but we will fail. No matter how hard we try or even how far we get, we still come up short. **For all have sinned, and come short of the glory of God; (Romans 3:23)** Solomon summed it up when he said, **For there is not a just man upon earth, that doeth good, and sinneth not. (Ecclesiastes 7:20)**

Paul says, **that the promise by faith of Jesus Christ might be given to them that believe. (Galatians 3:22b)** Even though we are hemmed in by sin and there is no way we can obey its commands, there is yet hope. Paul says the promise **might be given to them that believe.** Paul brings us back to that word **believe.** The word **believe** comes from the Greek *"pisteuo"* and simply means *"to have faith."* Paul has already argued and proved that faith is how Abraham was saved.

> **Even as Abraham believed God, and it was accounted to him for righteousness. (Galatians 3:6)**

We can't keep the law, but if we will believe we can be saved. Like Abraham believed God, and it was accounted to him for righteousness, we too can put our trust in the finished work of Christ and receive imputed righteousness.

> **For he hath made him to be sin for us, who knew no sin; that we might be made the righteousness of God in him. (2 Corinthians 5:21)**

When we take God at His word and call upon Him for forgiveness and salvation, He extends His grace, forgives our sin, justifies us, adopts us into His family and gives us life eternal.

THE POINTING OF THE LAW

Wherefore the law was our schoolmaster to bring us unto Christ, that we might be justified by faith" (Galatians 3:24). Noah Webster defines a **"schoolmaster"** as *"The man who presides over and teaches a school; a teacher, instructor or preceptor of a school."* In Paul's day the schoolmaster was a servant who had been given the responsibility of seeing that his Master's children were properly trained and educated. Paul lifts the work of a schoolmaster out of the culture of his day and uses it as an illustration of the law's relationship to Christ and sinner. The law reveals the holy and righteous character of God, the sinfulness and depravity of man, the need for a Saviour, and then points us to that Saviour. In other words, the law was designed to teach man his sinfulness and inadequacy to satisfy a Holy God. Thus, causing him to trust in Christ and be justified by faith.

THE PURVIEW OF THE LAW

Once the law has done its work and brought us to Christ we are no longer under its condemnation. Paul lists several benefits of being a child of God.

Our Pardon

But after that faith is come, we are no longer under a schoolmaster. (Galatians 3:25) Once salvation is realized the new believer has a whole different relationship with the law. Remember the context. Paul has used the illustration of children who were in school and subject to the schoolmaster. Before salvation we were disobedient children under the constraint and condemnation of the law. However, now that we are saved, we are obedient children who have graduated from the school of the law and are now under grace. We are no longer rebellious children who need the constant supervision of the schoolmaster, but rather children of God under His grace.

> **Then said Jesus to those Jews which believed on him, If ye continue in my word, then are ye my disciples indeed; And ye shall know the truth, and the truth shall make you free. They answered him, We be Abraham's seed, and were never in bondage to any man: how sayest thou, Ye shall be made free? Jesus answered them, Verily, verily, I say unto you, Whosoever committeth sin is the servant of sin. And the servant abideth not in the house for ever: but the Son abideth ever. If the Son therefore shall make you free, ye shall be free indeed. (John 8:31-36)**

It must be noted that freedom from the law is not the liberty to forsake righteousness and live as one pleases. **And I will walk at liberty: for I seek thy precepts. (Psalms 119:45)** Paul is in no way advocating a lascivious lifestyle. He is teaching us that rather than rebellious children, we have grown up and graduated to practice what we learned in school. Before our justification the law was over us like a school teacher, constantly teaching us what God required and condemning us for our failure to meet His requirement. However, the law has no authority over us once we come to Christ. Remember, the law can't justify us because we are incapable of keeping it. When we come to Christ by faith, He graciously forgives us and eternally justifies us. Therefore, the child of God is free from the law in the sense that he does not have to obey the law in order to maintain his justification.

Our Privilege

For ye are all the children of God by faith in Christ Jesus. (Galatians 3:26) Here is a wonderful truth that ought to warm and stir our hearts. We are **children of God.** We have been born again. **But as many as received him, to them gave he power to become the sons of God, even to them that believe on his name: (John 1:12)** If you have come to Christ for forgiveness, you are His child and He is your Father.

> **Behold, what manner of love the Father hath bestowed upon us, that we should be called the sons of God: therefore the world knoweth us not, because it knew him not. Beloved, now are we the sons of God, and it doth not yet appear what we shall be: but we know that, when he shall appear, we shall be like him; for we shall see him as he is. (1 John 3:1-2)**

Notice, John does not say, "We shall be sons of God." He does not say, "We hope to be the sons of God." He says, **Now are we the sons of God.** The moment a sinner turns to Christ, he is forgiven and born into the family of God. He is forever a child of God. Because we are children of God we have a new Father, a new Family, new Fortune and a new Future.

Our Placement

For as many of you as have been baptized into Christ have put on Christ. (Galatians 3:27) This verse describes two events.

First, there is a **_Putting In_**. **For as many of you as have been baptized into Christ... (Galatians 3:27a)** There are those who teach that a child of God does not necessarily receive the Holy Spirit at the time of salvation—that the Spirit may or may not come sometime later. This is their take on the "Baptism of the Holy Spirit." They are famous for asking, "Have you been baptized with the Holy Spirit?" Every born again child of God can answer that question with an absolute "yes." Paul wrote:

> **For by one Spirit are we all baptized into one body, whether we be Jews or Gentiles, whether we be bond or free; and have been all made to drink into one Spirit. (1 Corinthians 12:13)**

According to the Scriptures, how many of the Corinthian believers were baptized in the Spirit? The answer is clear! **"For by one Spirit are we ALL baptized."** The teaching that one must reach some mystical pinnacle of holiness to be baptized with the Holy Spirit is false. All of the Corinthian believers were baptized by the Holy Ghost. They certainly were not the most holy bunch around. In fact they were just the opposite! They were carnal (1 Corinthians 3). They were allowing immorality in their midst (1 Corinthians 5). They were at odds with one another even to the point of going to the law against one another (1 Corinthians 6). They were fighting and quarreling with one another (1 Corinthians 11-12). They were abusing the Lord's table, some to the point that God had to judge them and take their life (1 Corinthians 11). They were a self-centered, self-seeking, worldly people with a miserable testimony. Yet, the Bible says that they **ALL** were baptized by the Spirit of God.

The word **baptized** comes from the Greek *"baptizo"* and means to *"immerse"* or *"dip."* It is a word that was used in the secular world of dyeing a garment by dipping it into the dye. The idea is that of complete immersion. To be baptized in the Holy Spirit is to be immersed into the body of Christ. Every Christian receives the Holy Spirit at the moment of conversion.

> **In whom ye also trusted, after that ye heard the word of truth, the gospel of your salvation: in whom also after that ye believed, ye were sealed with that holy Spirit of promise. (Ephesians 1:13)**

Not only does every believer receive the Holy Spirit, but He comes permanently. The baptism of the Holy Spirit is the act whereby the believer is placed into the body of Christ.

Second, there is a **<u>Putting On</u>**. Paul speaks of having ... **put on Christ. (Galatians 3:27b)** The words **put on** come from the Greek *"endyo"* and means *"to clothe with."* So then to **put on Christ** is to clothe ourselves with Christ. How do we accomplish this? Paul said:

> **That ye put off concerning the former conversation the old man, which is corrupt**

> according to the deceitful lusts; And be renewed in the spirit of your mind; And that ye put on the new man, which after God is created in righteousness and true holiness. (Ephesians 4:22-24)
>
> But now ye also put off all these; anger, wrath, malice, blasphemy, filthy communication out of your mouth. Lie not one to another, seeing that ye have put off the old man with his deeds; And have put on the new man, which is renewed in knowledge after the image of him that created him. (Colossians 3:8-10)

In the terminology of putting off and putting on Paul compared the Christian life to stripping off the filthy clothes of a sinful past and putting on the white robes of Christ's righteousness. So to **put on Christ** is to strip ourselves of the sins and habits of the flesh and live the way He lived.

Our Position

> There is neither Jew nor Greek, there is neither bond nor free, there is neither male nor female: for ye are all one in Christ Jesus. (Galatians 3:28)

This speaks of unity and equality. We are one in Christ. Our position in Christ surpasses all racial, social and gender boundaries. We are all one in Him.

Our Promise

> And if ye be Christ's, then are ye Abraham's seed, and heirs according to the promise. (Galatians 3:29)

Just as Abraham received eternal life by faith, so do we. When we come to Christ we are placed in Christ and being in Christ makes us a descendant of Abraham and therefore an heir of the promise of justification. **And the scripture, foreseeing that God would justify the heathen through faith, preached before the gospel unto Abraham, saying, In thee shall all nations be blessed. (Galatians 3:8)**

Coming Of Age
Galatians 4:1-7

In chapter 3 Paul used the example of God's covenant promise to Abraham as proof that salvation is by grace through faith. In this section he goes on to develop that truth. Paul uses the Jewish custom of the adoption of sons as a picture of the spiritual adoption of the children of God. Paul draws upon this custom to illustrate our relationship with Christ.

THE ASSOCIATION WITH SERVANTS

All believers are spiritual heirs. **And if ye be Christ's, then are ye Abraham's seed, and heirs according to the promise. (Galatians 3:29)** As a child of God we have inherited the promises of the Abrahamic covenant (Galatians 3:14,16,18).

The Children

Now I say, That the heir, as long as he is a child, differeth nothing from a servant, though he be lord of all; (Galatians 4:1) Paul uses the illustration of an heir receiving his inheritance to point out that the bondage of the law preceded the spiritual adulthood of grace. An heir does not receive his inheritance until the benefactor dies or until he reaches a stipulated age. The heir will one day be **lord of all.** But **as long as he is a child...** he **differeth nothing from a servant.** Even an heir does not have liberty as a child. In fact, he differs little from a servant even though one day he will own and rule everything.

The Constraint

But is under tutors and governors until the time appointed of the father. (Galatians 4:2) The child though he be an heir, has no liberty, but is under the authority of **tutors and governors**. Fathers would charge capable servants with the responsibly caring for and educating their children. The child, even though he was an heir, was under the authority of these tutors and governors until **the time appointed**.

The words **time appointed** are from the Greek *"prothesmia"* and speaks of a *"predetermined time."* It carries the idea of being *"fixed beforehand."* No sensible father would give millions of dollars to an infant or a child. However, he puts the money into a trust fund to be released when his children reach a certain age and have been trained and tutored in the ways of life. Paul is still drawing from the illustration of a Jewish son becoming an adult. A Jewish boy receives his Bar Mitzvah at the age of 12 or 13. At that time he is declared a son and legally considered as an adult. At that time the son was no longer just a promisee to the inheritance, but he possesses the inheritance. In the same way God had predetermined a certain time in history when He would send forth His Son to redeem man from under the law. As a result, we no longer operate under the promise of an inheritance, but possess the inheritance when we come to Christ.

> **Blessed *be* the God and Father of our Lord Jesus Christ, which according to his abundant mercy hath begotten us again unto a lively hope by the resurrection of Jesus Christ from the dead, To an inheritance incorruptible, and undefiled, and that fadeth not away, reserved in heaven for you, Who are kept by the power of God through faith unto salvation ready to be revealed in the last time. (1 Peter 1:3-5)**

Even so we, when we were children, were in bondage under the elements of the world: (Galatians 4:3) Paul compares the nation of Israel to a child being trained. They were in bondage under the elements of the world just as a child being trained in the basics of life. The word **bondage** is from the Greek word *"douloo"* and means *"to be under the authority of another."* Before salvation we were like children under tutors and governors. We had no liberty. We were bound and held by the law. The word **elements** is from the Greek word *"stoicheion"* and refers to basic and elementary truths. The law with its requirements, ceremonies and Holy days served as the basic elementary schoolmaster that trained us and brought us to the adoption into the family of God.

THE ARRIVAL OF THE SAVIOUR

But when the fulness of the time was come, God sent forth his Son, made of a woman, made under the law, To redeem them that were under the law, that we might receive the adoption of sons. (Galatians 4:4-5) Paul is drawing a comparison of law and grace to childhood and sonship. Before Christ came, God's people were required to make offerings and sacrifices according to the law. This they did in obedience as they longed and waited for the promised Messiah. Once Christ came, He perfectly satisfied and fulfilled the demands of the law and all those who put their trust in Him are declared sons and adopted into the God's family.

The Moment Of His Coming

But when the fulness of the time was come... (Galatians 4:4a) The fullness of time is the time that God appointed (Galatians 4:2).This was all according to God's timing **Who worketh all things after the counsel of his own will... (Ephesians 1:11)** Just as the human father selected a date at which his son would receive the full rights of sonship, our Heavenly Father determined a time when the world would pass from its childhood under the law to sonship under grace. The events of Christ's incarnation, death, and resurrection marked the change from the dispensation of law to the age of grace.

The Means Of His Coming

God... (Galatians 4:4b) It was God the father Who sent Jesus to redeem sinners. Every aspect of salvation began with God. It wasn't religion, nor was it a denomination, but it was by Divine providence. God made the first move. **We love him, because he first loved us. (1 John 4:19)** We did not send for Christ, but God sent Christ to us!

The Miracle Of His Coming

Jesus was **... made of a woman, made under the law, (Galatians 4:4d)** Christ as born as a descendant of David.

The word **made** comes from *"ginomia"* and carries the idea of a *"transition from one state or form to another."* Paul uses the same terminology in the book of Romans. **Concerning his Son Jesus Christ our Lord, which was made of the seed of David according to the flesh. (Romans 1:3)** This is what happened at the Virgin Birth when the Christ took on a human nature. Notice He does not say, He was born of the seed of David, but He was **made of the seed of David according to the flesh.** John also used the same expression, **And the Word was made flesh, and dwelt among us, and we beheld his glory, the glory as of the only begotten of the Father, full of grace and truth. (John 1:14)** He was not born flesh but made flesh. Ordinary humans are born flesh every day, that requires no miracle. But Jesus Christ was made flesh. This is the Virgin Birth. This is what theologians often refer to as the Hypostatic union. Jesus Christ was 100% man and 100% God. Christ did not simply become human, but became a unique person, fully God, and at the same time, fully man.

The Mission Of His Coming

We are told that **God sent forth his Son (Galatians 4:4c)** The words **sent forth** are from the Greek word *"exapostello"* and means *"sent one."* The idea is that of sending one forth as a *"commissioned emissary or messenger."* Jesus came to earth as a messenger with a commission. The next verse tells us what His commission was.

To redeem them that were under the law, that we might receive the adoption of sons. (Galatians 4:5) Jesus came to provide what the law could not. Jesus redeems us from the curse and condemnation of the law. The word redeem is from the Greek *"exagorazo"* and means *"to ransom or rescue by paying a satisfactory price."* The word was used in the Bible times of purchasing a slave from the auction block. That slave was in bondage. He had nothing. He could not purchase his own freedom. What a picture of sinful mankind. A slave to sin and unable to obtain freedom. The sinner himself cannot make a satisfactory payment for his sin. The curse of the law rests heavy upon us all. Before Christ we were under the bondage of sin. **Cursed is every one that continueth not in all things which are written in the book of the law to do them. (Galatians 3:10)** But Christ stepped in and paid the redemptive price and redeemed us. Jesus Christ purchased redemption for man by paying the price demanded and satisfying the demands of the law. The purchase price was His blood. **Forasmuch as ye know that ye were not redeemed with corruptible things, as silver and gold, from your vain conversation received by tradition from your fathers; But with the precious blood of Christ, as of a lamb without blemish and without spot. (1 Peter 1:18-19)**

THE ADOPTION OF SONS

Now Paul takes this wonderful truth of adoption and drives it home to our hearts.

The Evidence Of Adoption

And because ye are sons, God hath sent forth the Spirit of his Son into your hearts, crying, Abba, Father. (Galatians 4:6) Paul says, **And because ye are sons...** Now that Christ has come, fulfilled the demands of the Law and redeemed us from its penalty, we are no longer servants, we are sons. We are no longer under the Law and it is no longer our schoolmaster. We are children of God with the full rights of sonship. There are three results of sonship which confirm that we are children of God.

First, the **_Provision Of The Spirit_**. **God hath sent forth the Spirit of his Son... (Galatians 4:6b)** At the very moment of salvation God gives the Holy Spirit. It is at this moment that the natural man has become a spiritual man. This is called regeneration. **Not by works of righteousness which we have done, but according to his mercy he saved us, by the washing of regeneration, and renewing of the Holy Ghost. (Titus 3:5)** Noah Webster defines regeneration as *"Reproduction; the act of producing anew."* Our first birth was the result of a generation from our parents. The second birth is a regeneration. That is we are born again. It is a spiritual birth from the Holy Spirit as He imparts to us new spiritual life. Paul said to the Corinthians, **Therefore if any man be in Christ, he is a new creature: old things are passed away; behold, all things are become new. (2 Corinthians 5:17)** We are a new creature. Not the same old man. The new creature in Christ is a new life with new desires. Regeneration effects a change in our nature. We became **partakers of the divine nature. (2 Peter 1:4)**

Second, the **_Placing Of The Spirit_**. Paul goes on to say, **into your hearts. (Galatians 4:6c)** Not only does the Holy Spirit come from the Father, but He indwells us. He takes up residence within the believer's heart. When Jesus was preparing His disciples for His departure, He said:

> **And I will pray the Father, and he shall give you another Comforter, that he may abide with you for ever; Even the Spirit of truth; whom the world cannot receive, because it seeth him not, neither knoweth him: but ye know him; for he dwelleth with you, and shall be in you. (John 14:16-17)**

You will notice Jesus said that the Holy Spirit **shall be in you.** The Holy Spirit indwelling the child of God was new to the Church. The Spirit's presence in the Old Testament was much different than in the New. They were not permanently indwelt by the Spirit as we are. He came upon God's people to anoint and empower them for a specific calling, but they were not indwelt nor was His presence permanent. Of Saul the Bible says, **But the Spirit of the LORD departed from Saul... (1 Samuel 16:14)** The same is true of Samson. The Bible says, **... he wist not that the LORD was departed from him. (Judges 16:20)** After his sin with Bathsheba, David prayed **... take not thy holy spirit from me. (Psalms 51:11)** The fact is that Old Testament saints could lose the presence and anointing of the Holy Spirit.

However, in this dispensation of grace, the Church age, God gives us the Holy Spirit with the guarantee of His abiding presence.

> **That we should be to the praise of his glory, who first trusted in Christ. In whom ye also trusted, after that ye heard the word of truth, the gospel of your salvation: in whom also after that ye believed, ye were sealed with that holy Spirit of promise, Which is the earnest of our inheritance**

until the redemption of the purchased possession, unto the praise of his glory. (Ephesians 1:12-14)

This is a powerful passage of Scripture. The Holy Spirit is described as the **earnest of our inheritance. (Ephesians 1:14)** The word **earnest** comes from *"arrabon"* and speaks of *"a pledge or a guarantee."* The word is a legal and commercial term that refers to a down payment made as a pledge of full payment. It is the guarantee of the purchaser's promise and intent to follow through on the entire transaction. The Holy Spirit's presence in our heart and life is God's guarantee that He is going to complete the transaction. **Being confident of this very thing, that he which hath begun a good work in you will perform it until the day of Jesus Christ: (Philippians 1:6)**

This word of God emphasizes the permanence of the Spirit's indwelling. **And grieve not the holy Spirit of God, whereby ye are sealed unto the day of redemption. (Ephesians 4:30)** Sealed for how long? The text says, **unto the day of redemption.** The **day of redemption** speaks of the finalization of salvation when even the body is redeemed. The soul is redeemed now, but the body will not be redeemed and delivered until the rapture. **And not only they, but ourselves also, which have the firstfruits of the Spirit, even we ourselves groan within ourselves, waiting for the adoption, to wit, the redemption of our body. (Romans 8:23)** The body is not redeemed yet. However, the seal of the Spirit guarantees our full and complete redemption.

God put the Holy Spirit permanently in the heart of the believer because New Testament Christianity is a heart religion. It is not something that is attained or lived by a set of rigid rules and regulation. Such a religion is legalism and produces nothing but bondage and defeat. The law could only affect and attempt to govern the external, but the Holy Spirit works from within the heart. The Bible says, **For as he thinketh in his heart, so is he... (Proverbs 23:7)** Life is lived from the heart. The heart is the decision-making center of life, the source of motives, the seat of the passions, the place where thoughts are conceived, and the center of the conscience. It is the place where life makes up its mind. Therefore, the Holy Spirit takes up His residence there and works to change and guide us. Jesus said, **But the Comforter, which is the Holy Ghost, whom the Father will send in my name, he shall teach you all things, and bring all things to your remembrance, whatsoever I have said unto you. (John 14:26)**

Third, the **<u>Proclamation Of The Spirit</u>**. The Holy Spirit comes into our hearts **... crying, Abba, Father. (Galatians 4:6d)** Notice here it is not the believer, but the Spirit that cries out to God. From the moment of His indwelling, the Spirit is crying out to God on our behalf (Romans 8:26). But praise be to God, because of our new relationship with Him we too can cry **Abba, Father. For ye have not received the spirit of bondage again to fear; but ye have received the Spirit of adoption, whereby we cry, Abba, Father. (Romans 8:15)** Not only is there a new standing as a child of God, but we also have a new relationship. The word **Abba** is the Aramaic word for *"Father."* It is similar to the English word

"Daddy or Papa," a term of endearment used by small children in addressing their fathers. Jesus used this term when praying in the garden of Gethsemane. **And he said, Abba, Father, all things are possible unto thee; take away this cup from me: nevertheless not what I will, but what thou wilt. (Mark 14:36)** It is a term that overflows with the thoughts of love, grace, and compassion. It vividly expresses the personal and intimate relationship we have with God. Because of God's adoption we are no longer servants bound by legalism but sons enjoying liberty in Christ.

The Enjoyment Of Adoption

Wherefore thou art no more a servant, but a son; and if a son, then an heir of God through Christ. (Galatians 4:7) Because we have been moved from servant to son, every believer is an **heir of God through Christ.** The law offered no inheritance. As believers we are heirs according to promise, not heirs according to works. Remember the context. Paul has been refuting the Judaizers and explaining that works and law never lead to salvation, but bondage and disappointment. A religion of works produces slavery, but grace produces sons **and if a son, then an heir of God through Christ.** Peter said:

> **Blessed be the God and Father of our Lord Jesus Christ, which according to his abundant mercy hath begotten us again unto a lively hope by the resurrection of Jesus Christ from the dead, To an inheritance incorruptible, and undefiled, and that fadeth not away, reserved in heaven for you, (1 Peter 1:3-4)**

As sons we are guaranteed an inheritance. Paul told the Roman believers, **And if children, then heirs; heirs of God, and joint-heirs with Christ; if so be that we suffer with him, that we may be also glorified together. (Romans 8:17)** Because of our new relationship with God as His children, we are **heirs of God**. An **inheritance** is wealth that one receives as a member of a family. Not only are we an heir of God, but we are also **joint-heirs with Christ.** Jesus said, **All things that the Father hath are mine… (John 16:15)** As joint-heirs we share in everything that God the Father has given to Jesus Christ. If we have the Son, we have everything.

The Pitfalls Of Legalism
Galatians 4:8-20

Paul has well argued that the believer has been freed from the bondage of the law and adopted into the family of God as a son. We are no longer a servant under the law, but hold a far greater position as a son with liberty. However, the Judaizers had managed to snare many of these believers and draw them back into legalism. Legalism is detrimental to the Christian life. Paul points out several pitfalls of legalism.

THE SLAVERY OF LEGALISM

Legalism enslaves the believer. The Christian's life is not designed to be lived as a slave under the rigid rules of a slave master, but rather as a son under the care of a loving Father. **If the Son therefore shall make you free, ye shall be free indeed. (John 8:36)** There is no way to enjoy our freedom as a son when we are fettered as a slave.

However, it must be understood that Christian liberty is not the freedom to live any way we want to. Nor is it the freedom to ignore the clear commands of God's word. Jesus said, **If ye continue in my word, then are ye my disciples indeed; And ye shall know the truth, and the truth shall make you free. (John 8:31-32)** Liberty is always based upon the Word of God. **And I will walk at liberty: for I seek thy precepts. (Psalm 119:45)** Christian liberty does not ignore the moral law of God. Law and liberty go hand in hand. You cannot separate one from the other.

When Paul refuted legalism he wasn't saying that we could scrap the law and live for the world. Paul was dealing with the Judaizers who made the law a requirement for salvation. Legalism says that Christ died for our sins, but that we still need to follow the dietary and ceremonial laws and observe the holy days of the Old Covenant in order to be right with God. That's legalism! Endeavoring to live and promote holiness is not legalism.

Their Pitiful Past

Howbeit then, when ye knew not God, ye did service unto them which by nature are no gods. (Galatians 4:8) Paul points them back to their pre-conversion condition. He says, **when ye knew not God.** That is in their ignorance when they didn't know any better so they **did service unto them which by nature are no gods.** Paul reminds them that before they were saved, they were under the bondage of idolatry. In their ignorance they didn't know the true God so they served whatever came down the pike. Man is a religious creature, He was made to worship and he will worship someone or something. Hence, all of the idolatry that exists in the world.

Jesus Christ is not simply added to one's pantheon of gods, instead a person must turn from all others to Christ alone. This was the testimony of the Thessalonian believers. They had **... turned to God from idols to serve the living and true God; (1 Thessalonians 1:9)** Jesus is the only way to Heaven. When one comes to Christ he must do so with the conviction that He alone saves and that there is no other. Jesus said:

> He that believeth on him is not condemned: but
> he that believeth not is condemned already,

> because he hath not believed in the name of the only begotten Son of God. (John 3:18)
>
> ... I am the way, the truth, and the life: no man cometh unto the Father, but by me. (John 14:6)

In the book of Acts Peter declared.

> Neither is there salvation in any other: for there is none other name under heaven given among men, whereby we must be saved. (Acts 4:12)

The Apostle John said:

> He that hath the Son hath life; and he that hath not the Son of God hath not life. (1 John 5:12)

The Galatians had once served idols because they didn't know any better. They were **without God. (Ephesians 2:12)** They operated, **... in the vanity of their mind, Having the understanding darkened, being alienated from the life of God through the ignorance that is in them, because of the blindness of their heart: (Ephesians 4:17-18)** Such is the sad condition of multitudes today.

Their Present Position

But now, after that ye have known God, or rather are known of God... (Galatians 4:9a) To know God and be known of God speaks of a personal relationship. The gospel had been preached and they had turned from their sin and idols to the true and living God. They knew God and God knew them. Christianity is a relationship, not a religion.

> Not every one that saith unto me, Lord, Lord, shall enter into the kingdom of heaven; but he that doeth the will of my Father which is in

heaven. **Many will say to me in that day, Lord, Lord, have we not prophesied in thy name? and in thy name have cast out devils? and in thy name done many wonderful works? And then will I profess unto them, I never knew you: depart from me, ye that work iniquity. (Matthew 7:21-23)**

Notice that these people where religious. They addressed Jesus as **Lord**. They had **prophesied** and **cast out devils** and had **done many wonderful works** in His name. Yet, Jesus commanded them to depart and declared their works to be nothing more than iniquity. The main thing was missing. Jesus said, **I never knew you.** They had religion, but they didn't have a relationship with Christ.

When the Galatians worshiped idols **they knew not God … (Galatians 4:8)** The word **knew** comes from the Greek *"eido"* and carries the idea of *"perceiving, being aware of."* But when Paul says in verse 9 **ye have known God**, he uses the Greek word *"ginosko"* for **known**. This word *"ginosko"* speaks of a personal knowledge that comes from experience. Jesus said, **And this is life eternal, that they might know thee the only true God, and Jesus Christ, whom thou hast sent. (John 17:3)**. These Galatian believers knew God and He knew them. These were saved people.

Their Perilous Practice

… how turn ye again to the weak and beggarly elements, whereunto ye desire again to be in bondage? Ye observe days, and months, and times, and years. (Galatians 4:9b-10) It is tragically possible for a believer to get sidetracked by false doctrine. These Galatians knew better. They had heard and embraced the truth. They knew what was right and yet the Judaizers had deceived them and as a result they had returned to bondage. How could that happen? They were saved, but they were not serious about the things of God. Paul addressed this back in chapter three,

> **O foolish Galatians, who hath bewitched you, that ye should not obey the truth, before whose eyes Jesus Christ hath been evidently set forth, crucified among you? (Galatians 3:1)**

Paul uses the word **foolish** twice in reference to the Galatians. The word **foolish** comes from *"anoetos"* and carries the idea of *"ignorant, no understanding, unwise."* It speaks of someone who is lacking in discernment. They had been taught the truth, but had failed to examine the teaching of the Judaizers in the light of the truth. As a result, the Judaizers lead them out of truth and into bondage. Paul further states that they had been **bewitched**. The word **bewitched** comes from *"baskaino"* and means *"to charm or fascinate by false representation."* It carries the idea of bringing evil upon someone by using trickery and flattery. The Galatian believers had been fully instructed in the doctrine and details of the gospel of Jesus Christ. Yet they had been tricked and deceived into turning back **to the weak and beggarly elements** and gone back into **bondage**. They were back to observing **days, and months, and times, and years.** The legalists had charmed the Galatians into legalism.

Their Perplexed Preacher

I am afraid of you, lest I have bestowed upon you labour in vain. (Galatians 4:11) Their foolishness struck fear in Paul's heart. There is not a pastor in America who doesn't know how Paul felt. The word **labour** comes from the Greek *"kopiao"* and means *"to work hard, to be weary."* The idea is that of laboring to the point of exhaustion. As a faithful preacher Paul had labored diligently among the Galatians winning them to Christ and teaching them the truth. Paul was fearful that his labor was in vain. The word **vain** comes from the Greek *"eike"* and means *"to be idle, without effect."* It carries the idea of failure. For them to forsake that truth and go back into Judaism would be a failure.

Brethren, I beseech you, be as I am; for I am as ye are: ye have not injured me at all. (Galatians 4:12) Paul uses the word **beseech** over twenty times in this letter. It means *"to invite or entreat"* and carries the idea of begging. When Paul makes the appeal **be as I am**, he is reminding them that he has been faithful to the gospel of grace and he's begging them to do the same.

Paul says, **for I am as ye are...** The Galatians were Gentiles and Paul is reminding them that he had forsaken Judaism to become a Christian. He had realized that there was no salvation in the law and by grace he turned to Christ alone for salvation. Paul pleads with the Galatians to abandon the law and trust Christ alone.

Paul says, **ye have not injured me at all.** He is assuring them that his rebuke is not personal but a matter of principle. It is not a personal fight, but they are in error and must be corrected.

THE SCORN OF LEGALISM

Most folks don't take rebuke well. The old flesh kicks in, pride flares up and there's trouble. Unfortunately, the

Galatians had rejected Paul's message and even to the point that they were treating him as an enemy. Having just assured them that this was not a personal issue Paul goes on to remind them of their past relationship in the Lord.

He Reminds Them Of Their Conversion

Ye know how through infirmity of the flesh I preached the gospel unto you at the first. (Galatians 4:13) Paul takes them back to when he first preached the gospel to them and reminded them that he did so through an **infirmity of the flesh.** The word **infirmity** comes from *"astheneia"* and means *"feebleness; disease, sickness, weakness."* We are not told exactly what Paul's infirmity was, but it was obviously something that greatly hindered him. Our context suggests that Paul's infirmity had to do with his eyesight. A few verses later Paul says, **... if it had been possible, ye would have plucked out your own eyes, and have given them to me. (Galatians 4:15b)** Towards the end of this epistle he says, **Ye see how large a letter I have written unto you with mine own hand. (Galatians 6:11)** Paul reminds the Galatians how he came to Galatia and even though hindered by a great physical ailment, he preached the gospel and many of them were saved.

He Reminds Them Of Their Confidence

And my temptation which was in my flesh ye despised not, nor rejected; but received me as an angel of God, even as Christ Jesus. (Galatians 4:14) Paul's infirmity did not turn the Galatians off to the gospel message. Instead they received him **... as an angel of God, even as Christ**

Jesus. They **despised not, nor rejected** Paul, but accepted him and treated him as a messenger of God. They cared for and respected him as they would have **Christ Jesus** had He personally come to them. Isn't it amazing how quick folks can turn on the preacher when he has to rebuke someone or preaches something they don't like.

He Reminds Them Of Their Compassion

Where is then the blessedness ye spake of? for I bear you record, that, if it had been possible, ye would have plucked out your own eyes, and have given them to me. (Galatians 4:15) The word **blessedness** comes from the Greek *"makarismos"* and means *"the attribution of good fortune."* When they were first saved the Galatians praised God and exhibited great joy. Paul asks, **Where is then the blessedness ye spake of?** In other words, What happened to all that joy and happiness? The implication here is that legalism destroys Christian joy and friendships. Legalism sucks the joy out of Christianity.

THE STRIFE OF LEGALISM

Am I therefore become your enemy, because I tell you the truth? (Galatians 4:16) Oh how much things had changed! They no longer considered Paul a friend, but an enemy. Why? Paul says, **because I tell you the truth...** The very message that had brought them together, the truth, had now come between them. The gospel that once brought great joy to the Galatians, now irritated them. Paul was now considered an enemy because he stood on the truth. When folks don't like the message they almost always take it out on the messenger. Isn't it amazing that the Judaizers became their friends by telling them lies, but Paul became their enemy when he told the truth.

> **Reprove not a scorner, lest he hate thee: rebuke a wise man, and he will love thee. (Proverbs 9:8)**

The messenger they once loved and accepted as Christ, they now hated. When he first came they would have given him their eyes, now they wanted to give him the boot. Why? Because he told them the truth. He exposed their legalism.

They zealously affect you ... (Galatians 4:17a) The Judaizers were zealous in their attempts to infiltrate the Galatian Church with their legalism. The phrase **zealously affect** comes from *"zeloo"* and speaks of a *"passionate enthusiasm."* The idea is that of courting someone. When a man courts a lady he has to be at his best. He does everything he can to make her like him. That is what these legalists were doing. They were courting the Galatians.

Paul says, **but not well; yea, they would exclude you, that ye might affect them. (Galatians 4:17b)** Their affect wasn't for the good, but for the worse. Their courting was nothing more than manipulation designed to bewitch the Galatians. Paul warned, **they would exclude you, that ye might affect them.** They wanted to **exclude** the Galatians from God's grace and gain control over them for their own profit. They did not seek the good of the Galatians, but their own gain. This is how legalists works.

But it is good to be zealously affected always in a good thing... (Galatians 4:18a) Zeal is not a bad thing as long as it is about a **good thing**. They were zealous about the gospel of grace when Paul was with them and that was a good thing. Now they had lost their zeal for the gospel of grace.

... and not only when I am present with you. (Galatians 4:18b) If it's worth standing for when the preacher is around, it's worth standing for the rest of the time. Some folks get pretty excited when a big shot preacher shows up and mesmerizes the crowd with his oratory skills. They get all excited and fall on the altar making commitment after commitment. But it's not long before they lose their zeal and the fire is quenched. May we remember that our allegiance and faithfulness is to God and never contingent on the preachers presence.

Liberty Or Slavery
Galatians 4:19-31

Paul draws upon the Old Testament account of Sarah and Hagar to further illustrate his teaching concerning law and grace.

PAUL'S COMPASSION

My little children, of whom I travail in birth again until Christ be formed in you, I desire to be present with you now, and to change my voice; for I stand in doubt of you. (Galatians 4:19-20) Paul's compassion and concern for the Galatians is so heartfelt that he compares it to labor pains. Paul was as concerned for them now as he was before they had professed Christ. Paul was heartbroken over the sad spiritual condition of the Galatians. Because of their false doctrine and their unwillingness to change, Paul said ... **I stand in doubt of you.** Paul doubted their salvation. They had a profession, but no visible evidence that they were even saved. However, Paul had hope and longed to visit them to see **Christ ... formed** in them.

PAUL'S COMPARISON

Tell me, ye that desire to be under the law, do ye not hear the law? (Galatians 4:21) Verses 21 through 30 Paul uses an allegory to illustrate the difference between the law and grace.

For it is written, that Abraham had two sons, the one by a bondmaid, the other by a freewoman. (Galatians 4:22) God promised Abraham a son, but his wife Sarah was barren so she invented a plan whereby Abraham could father a son. As a result, Abraham fathered a child with Sarah's handmaid, Hagar. Hagar was the **bondmaid** and Sarah the **freewoman (Genesis 16-21).** God rejected Abraham and Sarah's pitiful attempt at fulfilling His promise. In His mercy, God miraculously gave Abraham and Sarah their son Isaac—the child of promise. Isaac was born of the **freewoman,** Sarah, and represents grace. Ishmael was born of the **bondmaid,** Hagar, and represents the law. Paul contrast these two women and uses them as an **allegory** to teach a lesson on law and grace.

But he who was of the bondwoman was born after the flesh; but he of the freewoman was by promise. (Galatians 4:23) Paul states that Hagar's son, Ishmael, **was born after the flesh**. That means that he was born entirely by the will of man. Ishmael was the result of Abraham and Sarah taking the promise of God into their own hands. Ismael was a product of unbelief. Isaac, however, was born by **promise**. As always, God delivered on His promise and Isaac was born as the unfailing promise of God.

Which things are an allegory: for these are the two covenants; the one from the mount Sinai, which gendereth to bondage, which is Agar. For this Agar is mount Sinai in Arabia, and answereth to Jerusalem which now is, and is in bondage with her children. But Jerusalem which is above is free, which is the mother of us all. (Galatians 4:24-26) These two women represent two covenants. One speaks of the law which makes the blessing dependent upon man carrying out his part of the covenant; the other is a covenant of promise in which the fulfillment rests entirely upon the grace of God. Isaac and Ishmael suggest the two conditions that result from these **two covenants**: the one of bondage; the other of freedom and liberty. Also, these two covenants are connected with Mount Sinai, where the law was given, and with Jerusalem which is above, from which grace is received.

For it is written, Rejoice, thou barren that bearest not; break forth and cry, thou that travailest not: for the desolate hath many more children than she which hath an husband. (Galatians 4:27) Again, Paul draws upon the Old Testament and quotes Isaiah 54:1. These words were originally given to encourage the Jewish exiles who were in bondage in Babylon. However, Paul applies it to the allegory to further illustrate the superiority of grace. Though Sarah's bareness seemingly hindered the fulfillment of God's promise to Abraham, she ultimately became the mother of more children than Hagar. Likewise Christianity is destined for greater glory as God calls out from among the Gentiles a bride for his name.

Now we, brethren, as Isaac was, are the children of promise. (Galatians 4:28) Paul explains to the Galatians that believers in Jesus are the **children of promise**. Like Isaac, Christians are born into the family of God by the miraculous regenerating power of the Holy Spirit. Once Abraham and Sarah, by faith, rested in the promise of God, Isaac was born. So, by faith one becomes a child of God through His promise to save anyone who will come to Him. The emphasis here is that, those who by faith come to Christ are the spiritual descendants of God's promise to Abraham.

But as then he that was born after the flesh persecuted him that was born after the Spirit, even so it is now. (Galatians 4:29) Paul continues with the account of Ishmael mocking Isaac (Genesis 21:8-10). This is where the Arab\Israeli conflict began and even continues to this very day. It cannot be denied that the Arab nations, for the most part, have persecuted Israel. Down through the ages, the Arabic peoples certainly have fought against Israel. However, Paul's application was to the Galatians who were suffering for their faith in Christ. Like the Arabs had persecuted the Jews, so the Jewish legalists were persecuting the Church.

Nevertheless what saith the scripture? Cast out the bondwoman and her son: for the son of the bondwoman shall not be heir with the son of the freewoman. (Galatians 4:30) Like Abraham rejected and cast out Hagar and Ishmael, it is the responsibility of New Testament believers to reject legalism. We must cast it out of our midst. Legalism and grace are direct opposites and cannot coexist together. There will never be harmony between the two. One contradicts the other.

PAUL'S CONCLUSION

So then, brethren, we are not children of the bondwoman, but of the free. (Galatians 4:31) Because we are saved by grace, we are not descendants of Hagar bound under the law. We are free in Christ and destined to enjoy the liberty that can be found only in Him. **If the Son therefore shall make you free, ye shall be free indeed. (John 8:36)**

Living In Liberty
Galatians 5:1-12

The Judaizers were pressuring the Galatians to return to the law. In this chapter circumcision had become an issue. The Galatians had been saved by the grace of God. However, they were being taught to return to the law to receive God's favor and maintain their Christian life. What they had started by grace they were attempting to finish by law. What had begun in the Spirit they were continuing by works of the flesh.

THE PRECIOUS LIBERTY

Stand fast therefore in the liberty wherewith Christ hath made us free, and be not entangled again with the yoke of bondage. (Galatians 5:1) Paul's challenge to the child of God here is concerning his freedom in Christ. Our liberty in Christ is a precious possession. He satisfied the law and paid the sin debt for every man. Paul gives us a two-fold responsibility concerning our liberty.

Stand Fast

Stand fast therefore in the liberty wherewith Christ hath made us free... (Galatians 5:1a) By the finished work of Jesus Christ upon Calvary's cross all who come to Him are forgiven, saved, and set free from sin and the law. **If the Son therefore shall make you free, ye shall be free indeed. (John 8:36)**

Paul commands us to **Stand fast** in our liberty. The word **stand** comes from the Greek *"steko"* and means just what it says, we are to **stand fast.** It is a word that suggests stability without wavering. It is in the perfect tense meaning that we are to take our stand and keep on standing. Christ has made us free and given us liberty, now we are to maintain our position.

Stay Free

Paul says, **...and be not entangled again with the yoke of bondage. (Galatians 5:1)** Notice Paul's terminology here. He warns them not to be **entangled** in legalism. The word entangled comes from *"enecho"* and is a trapping term that describes putting snares out to capture animals. The Judaizers were attempting to snare the Galatians with their legalism.

Paul further described this as the **yoke of bondage.** He uses the illustration of a yoke as worn by an ox. Just like an ox is bound and controlled by the yoke, the Galatians were in danger of becoming bound and governed by a religious system rather than the grace of God. All the law can do is keep us in bondage, demanding works we are incapable of performing and maintaining. The Christian life is received, lived and maintained by grace. It is a life that commences by grace and must continue by grace. Jesus said, **And ye shall know the truth, and the truth shall make you free. (John 8:32)**

THE POSSIBLE LOSS

Behold, I Paul say unto you, that if ye be circumcised, Christ shall profit you nothing. (Galatians 5:2) The

Galatians were waffling in their faith and going back to the works of the law to try and please God. Paul warns them of four consequences that would befall them if they did this.

A Serious Deficit

Paul says, ... **if ye be circumcised, Christ shall profit you nothing. (Galatians 5:2)** Their Saviour would be of no benefit to them if they insisted on observing the rites and ceremonies of the law instead of standing fast in the liberty that Christ had bestowed upon them. Their adherence to the law distracted them from the grace and glory of God. They were frustrating the grace of God with a divided heart. They had started out in Christ but now were trusting their works, thereby taking glory from Christ and giving it to the law and their ability to keep it. When the Christian relies upon the flesh he gets the glory instead of God and God has determined that **no flesh should glory in his presence. (1 Corinthians 1:29)** Christ will not share His glory with another. It is all of Christ or nothing. **Jesus said unto him, Thou shalt love the Lord thy God with all thy heart, and with all thy soul, and with all thy mind. (Matthew 22:37)** When the Christian attempts to operate under the power of the flesh he takes away from God's grace and Christ profits him nothing.

A Sinful Debtor

Any believer who departs from grace to operate in the flesh becomes a **debtor to do the whole law. (Galatians 5:2)** James said the same thing. **For whosoever shall keep the whole law, and yet offend in one point, he is guilty of all.**

(James 2:10) The point here is that one who is going to operate according to the law and attempt to please God with works of the flesh is duty bound to keep the whole law and a failure to do so would place themselves under the curse of the law. **For as many as are of the works of the law are under the curse: for it is written, Cursed is every one that continueth not in all things which are witten in the book of the law to do them. (Galatians 3:10)**

A Startling Default

Christ is become of no effect unto you ... (Galatians 5:4a) The words **no effect** come from the Greek *"apo"* and basically means *"separation, departure, cessation."* The idea is that of separating one object from another. When a believer embraces legalism he sets Christ aside. Grace and law, and faith and works do not mix.

A Sure Downfall

Paul said, **ye are fallen from grace. (Galatians 5:4b)** It is sad that many Bible teachers miss the point of this statement and falsely teach that it is possible for a saved person to sin and become lost. The Bible teaches that those who are truly saved **shall never perish**. By believing on Christ, the Christian receives a salvation that cannot be taken away or forfeited. Nothing can separate the child of God from the love of Christ. Those who hold to the Bible doctrine of eternal security are simply exercising faith in what God said. When Jesus said, **I will never leave thee, nor forsake thee. (Hebrews 13:5)**, we believe that. When He said, **All that the Father giveth me shall come to me; and**

him that cometh to me I will in no wise cast out. (John 6:37), we believe Him. When Jesus says, **And I give unto them eternal life; and they shall never perish, neither shall any man pluck them out of my hand (John 10:28)**, we take Him at His word.

What Paul is teaching here is that a believer who operates in his own power has deserted the principle of grace. He acts as if the grace of God has no part in his life. In other words, he abandons the grace of God and lives in his own power. He may make many claims to holiness and godliness. Claiming to pray, to preach, even appearing to do mighty works for God, but having failed of the grace of God by accomplishing everything in the flesh. One who operates this way has fallen from grace.

THE PRODUCTIVE LOVE

For we through the Spirit wait for the hope of righteousness by faith. For in Jesus Christ neither circumcision availeth any thing, nor uncircumcision; but faith which worketh by love. (Galatians 5:5-6) In these verses Paul explains that the New Testament believer is motivated by love rather than the law.

Our Power

Paul says, **For we through the Spirit ...** There it is! It is the Spirit-driven life as opposed to the flesh-driven life. The Christian who operates according to the flesh is not Spirit-led. If our accomplishments are gained in the flesh, the Spirit of God has no part in it. Then we are **fallen from grace. (Galatians 5:4)** Such a lifestyle is entirely of the flesh. Jesus made it clear that **... the flesh profiteth nothing. (John 6:63)** Anything the Christian accomplishes must be by the power and production of the Holy Spirit. **Not by might, nor by power, but by my spirit, saith the LORD of hosts. (Zechariah 4:6)**

Our Purity

Paul says that we **...wait for the hope of righteousness by faith. (Galatians 5:5b)** The Judaizers' hope was in their ceremony and ritual. They hoped to please God by their works. They were attempting to obey the law as a means of salvation. But the child of God does not serve to be saved, instead we serve because we are saved. It is not righteousness that we hope for, but the **hope of righteousness** which we have in Jesus Christ. As believers we already have imputed righteousness.

> **But to him that worketh not, but believeth on him that justifieth the ungodly, his faith is counted for righteousness. (Romans 4:5)**

God has imputed Christ's righteousness to the believer's account.

> **For he hath made him to be sin for us, who knew no sin; that we might be made the righteousness of God in him. (2 Corinthians 5:21)**

God sees us as righteous in Christ. Our imputed righteousness is positional, but the **hope of righteousness** that we wait for is perfect and final.

> **Beloved, now are we the sons of God, and it doth not yet appear what we shall be: but we know**

> that, when he shall appear, we shall be like him; for we shall see him as he is. (1 John 3:2)

When Christ comes in His glory every believer will be glorified. That's our hope!

Our Position

For in Jesus Christ neither circumcision availeth any thing, nor uncircumcision ... (Galatians 5:6a) The peril of legalism is bondage to religion rather than liberty in Jesus Christ. The legalistic Judaizers were pushing to have all Christians circumcised. God had instituted circumcision as a mark of His covenant with Abraham and his descendants (Genesis 17:10-12). The Jews however took great pride in the rite of circumcision. Circumcision had become a big issue in Galatia as well as in other places. Paul warned the Philippians:

> **Beware of dogs, beware of evil workers, beware of the concision. For we are the circumcision, which worship God in the spirit, and rejoice in Christ Jesus, and have no confidence in the flesh. (Philippians 3:2-3)**

Notice that Paul contrasts worshiping God in the Spirit with confidence in the flesh. Paul said, **We are the circumcision,** Paul is saying that we have the circumcision of Christ. Not the circumcision of the flesh, but of the heart. These are the true Christians who **worship God in the spirit.**

The Judaizers focused on work done on the flesh, but for the true Christian, God has done a work in the heart. God is not impressed by outward ceremonies and rituals, He desires inner change. Without an obedient heart, circumcision was a useless ritual. It was not the circumcision that made one right with God. It is the obedience from a pure heart that pleases God.

Circumcision apart from obedience was useless, and to these Judaizers it was just that—a useless ritual. An unsaved man could perform all the ceremonies and rituals of the law as well as a spiritual man, but they were still unsaved.

Paul warned the Jews in Rome, **For circumcision verily profiteth, if thou keep the law: but if thou be a breaker of the law, thy circumcision is made uncircumcision. (Romans 2:25)** Paul points out that circumcision is only profitable if the Jew keeps the whole law. However, if the Law is broken, even in one minute detail, the external symbol becomes worthless.

But he is a Jew, which is one inwardly; and circumcision is that of the heart, in the spirit, and not in the letter; whose praise is not of men, but of God. (Romans 2:29) Paul explains that circumcision was a symbol of what had happened inside of a man—in his heart. The Judaizers had missed their relationship with God and let the ceremony itself become their religion. The legalists prided themselves in their circumcision and keeping of the law, but in Christ circumcision has no meaning.

Our Production

Paul goes on to say, **... but faith which worketh by love. (Galatians 5:6b)** Notice the order of these words. It is **faith which worketh.** Faith always comes before works. Until a person is saved all of his works are **as filthy rags. (Isaiah 64:6)** We see here that faith not only *__Precedes Works__*, but saving faith also *__Produces Works__*. If it doesn't work, it is not saving faith. Works are not the root of salvation, they are the fruit. James wrote,

> **But wilt thou know, O vain man, that faith without works is dead? (James 2:20)**

A man who's faith produces no fruit is call a **vain man**. The word **vain** means *"empty, shallow."* It is an empty and shallow faith that claims to know God, but does not manifest itself in service to God. Genuine faith is seen in our work for God. Jesus said:

> **Let your light so shine before men, that they may see your good works, and glorify your Father which is in heaven. (Matthew 5:16)**

While salvation is apart from works, it is certainly unto works. Paul preached the same doctrine.

> **For we are his workmanship, created in Christ Jesus unto good works, which God hath before ordained that we should walk in them. (Ephesians 2:10)**

God's purpose in saving us goes beyond simply rescuing us from Hell. We are saved to serve.

Paul reminds us that we are motivated **by love. (Galatians 5:6c)** The law *__Commands Us To Work__*, but love *__Compels Us To Work__*. It's not arm-twisting, manipulation, guilt trips and legalism that motivates us. It is love. Jesus said, **If ye love me, keep my commandments. (John 14:15)** Our relationship with Christ is not law based, it is love based. The Christian life is not an ungoverned life, nor is it a life governed by a list of *"thou-shalt-nots."* Our Christian life is governed by our love for Jesus Christ. When Jesus said, **If ye love me, keep my commandments**, He was saying that the supreme proof of our relationship with Him is our obedience.

THE POWERFUL LESSON

Ye did run well; who did hinder you that ye should not obey the truth? (Galatians 5:7) Here is one of Paul's favorite metaphors. He likens the Christian life to a race. Paul used the same analogy with the Philippians, **I press toward the mark for the prize of the high calling of God in Christ Jesus. (Philippians 3:14)** Paul reminds the Galatians that they at one time ran well. They were on track with their eyes on the goal and committed to finishing the race.

But there was a problem! Paul asks, **... who did hinder you that ye should not obey the truth? (Galatians 5:7b)** They were running well and then something went wrong. Satan brought someone along to hinder them. The word **hinder** comes from the Greek *"anakopto"* and means *"to beat or drive back."* It is an Olympic phrase that described someone who cut across the track and shoved another runner off of the course. That is what had happened to the Galatians. The Judaizers had cut in front of them and threw them off course with their legalism.

This persuasion cometh not of him that calleth you. (Galatians 5:8) The word **persuasion** comes from the Greek *"peismone"* and is used only here in the New Testament. The idea is that the Galatians had been persuaded to abandon their faith. Paul further points out that God had no part in it. Legalism and bondage never come from God. He works by grace.

THE PERILOUS LEAVEN

A little leaven leaveneth the whole lump. (Galatians 5:9) Leaven is often used in the Word of God to illustrate corruption and impurity. When put in dough leaven has a permeating affect, working from within and spreading throughout the whole lump.

> **Another parable spake he unto them; The kingdom of heaven is like unto leaven, which a woman took, and hid in three measures of meal, till the whole was leavened. (Matthew 13:33)**
>
> **Purge out therefore the old leaven, that ye may be a new lump, as ye are unleavened. For even Christ our passover is sacrificed for us: (1 Corinthians 5:7)**
>
> **Then Jesus said unto them, Take heed and beware of the leaven of the Pharisees and of the Sadducees ... Then understood they how that he bade *them* not beware of the leaven of bread, but of the doctrine of the Pharisees and of the Sadducees. (Matthew 16:6, 12)**

Paul used leaven as an illustration of the corrupting influence that the Judaizers had on the Church at Galatia. No amount of heresy should ever be permitted to exist within a local church. It only takes a little sin or a little false doctrine to begin the leavening process that will soon permeate the whole.

THE PERVERTED LEADERS

I have confidence in you through the Lord, that ye will be none otherwise minded: but he that troubleth you shall bear his judgment, whosoever he be. And I, brethren, if I yet preach circumcision, why do I yet suffer persecution? then is the offence of the cross ceased. (Galatians 5:10-11) Paul had confidence that the Galatian believers would finally reject legalism and fully embrace the grace principle of Scripture. He further believed that the Judaizers would bear the judgment of God for troubling the Galatian Church with their legalism.

I would they were even cut off which trouble you. (Galatians 5:12) The words cut off come from the Greek *"apokopto"* and speaks of amputation. The idea is the removal of an infected limb so as to prohibit further disease. Paul used this word to express his desire that the Judaizers would be removed from the Galatian Church.

The War Within
Galatians 5:15-17

The Bible teaches that within every Christian are two opposite and opposing natures. These two natures constantly contend for the believer's will.

THE CLASH

But if ye bite and devour one another, take heed that ye be not consumed one of another. (Galatians 5:15) By way of introduction, let me say a few words about the clash that takes place when God's people walk in the flesh instead of the Spirit. When the flesh is in control unity is sacrificed and disruption occurs. Because of the Galatians' attempt to satisfy God by works of the flesh complete disunity had developed among them. Their fleshly conduct and desires had caused them to turn on one another. A lot of local Churches are like that. It is kind of like a traffic jam—everyone tooting their horn and trying to get out ahead of everyone else. Nothing good can come from a flesh driven life.

Paul uses the words, **bite** and **devour** in describing the Galatians' treatment of one another. These words, used as a metaphor, were taken by Paul from the actions of dogs and wild beasts to describe the way flesh driven people treat each other. The fleshly Galatians were just like a bunch of wild animals that bite, claw, and devour each other, fighting to the bitter end. What a sad description of God's people. A people who above all others should understand and practice the love of God. Jesus said, **A new commandment I give unto you, That ye love one another; as I have loved you, that ye also love one another. By this shall all men know that ye are my disciples, if ye have love one to another. (John 13:34-35)** We will deal more with this command later in this series.

THE CONTRAST

Walk in the Spirit, and ye shall not fulfil the lust of the flesh. (Galatians 5:16) Here we see the sharp contrast between the walking in the Spirit and fulfilling the lust of the flesh. It is important that we understand the teaching of God's Word concerning these two natures. When God saves us He does not eradicate the old depraved nature which we receive at our natural birth. God does, however, impart to the believer an absolutely new nature, born of the Holy Spirit of God.

The Depraved Nature

This is the old nature that man is born into the world with. This old nature is referred to as the **natural man**. Paul wrote, **But the natural man receiveth not the things of the Spirit of God: for they are foolishness unto him: neither can he know them, because they are spiritually discerned. (1 Corinthians 2:14)** It is a nature of depravity and corruption and delights in sin and wickedness. This old depraved and sinful nature is not eradicated in the new birth as some teach. The old nature remains in the believer and remains just as corrupt and depraved as always. The Bible sometimes refers to this old nature as the **old man**. Paul speaking to the Ephesian Church admonished them, **That ye put off concerning the former conversation the old man, which is corrupt according to the deceitful lusts. (Ephesians 4:22)** They were born again, blood washed children of God that Paul was talking to. But notice that Paul told them to put off the **old man**. The old man wasn't gone. He was still there and had to be dealt with according to the Word of God.

The old nature is not in subjection to the law of God. **Because the carnal mind is enmity against God: for it is not subject to the law of God, neither indeed can be. (Romans 8:7)** It is a nature that is an enemy of God and hates everything that is holy and decent. **For I know that in me (that is, in my flesh,) dwelleth no good thing: for to will is present with me; but how to perform that which is good I find not. (Romans 7:18)** It was the old depraved nature that Jeremiah was speaking of when he said, **The heart is deceitful above all things, and desperately wicked: who can know it? (Jeremiah 17:9)** Jesus was talking about the old depraved nature when He said, **From within, out of the heart of men, proceed evil thoughts, adulteries, fornication, murders, thefts, covetousness, wickedness, deceit, lasciviousness, an evil eye, blasphemy, pride, foolishness: all these evil things come from within, and defile the man. (Mark 7:21-23)** In his book, All Of Grace, Charles Haddon Spurgeon wrote:

> The old nature is very strong, and they have tried to curb and tame it; but it will not be subdued, and they find themselves, though anxious to be better, if anything growing worse

than before. The heart is so hard, the will is so obstinate, the passions are so furious, the thoughts are so volatile, the imagination is so ungovernable, the desires are so wild, that the man feels that he has a den of wild beasts within him, which will eat him up sooner than be ruled by him. We may say of our fallen nature what the Lord said to Job concerning Leviathan: Wilt thou play with him as with a bird? or wilt thou bind him for thy maidens? A man might as well hope to hold the north wind in the hollow of his hand as expect to control by his own strength those boisterous powers which dwell within his fallen nature.

The old nature was not altered or changed at salvation, neither can it be reformed. The Bible tells us that the only method for dealing with the old nature is crucifixion. Paul said, **I am crucified with Christ: nevertheless I live; yet not I, but Christ liveth in me: and the life which I now live in the flesh I live by the faith of the Son of God, who loved me, and gave himself for me. (Galatians 2:20)** Again, to the Romans, Paul wrote, **For if ye live after the flesh, ye shall die: but if ye through the Spirit do mortify the deeds of the body, ye shall live. (Romans 8:13)** The old nature must be put off. It can be crucified and controlled, but it cannot be reformed.

The Divine Nature

The Divine nature is given to man as the result of being born again. **Therefore if any man be in Christ, he is a new creature: old things are passed away; behold, all things are** become new. (2 Corinthians 5:17) Jesus said, **That which is born of the Spirit is spirit. (John 3:6)** This is the new birth when one becomes a **partaker of the divine nature. (2 Peter 1:4)** The new nature cannot and will not sin because it is born of God **Whosoever is born of God doth not commit sin; for his seed remaineth in him: and he cannot sin, because he is born of God. (1 John 3:9)** When the believer sins it is because he submits and succumbs to the old nature. Dr. H. A Ironside, wrote the following in his commentary on Colossians:

> When a person is converted, or regenerated, this carnal nature is not altered in the slightest degree; it is never improved or sanctified, either in whole or in part. In the cross of Christ, God has utterly condemned the old nature as too vile for improvement. The believer has received a new nature that is spiritual, the nature of the new man; and he is now responsible to walk in obedience to the Word of God, which appeals only to this new nature. Both the old and the new natures are in the believer and will be until the redemption of the body.
>
> It is true that the flesh, or the old nature, acts through the members of the body, but the body itself is not evil. However, every natural instinct and physical appetite, no matter how perfectly right and proper they may be when used as God intended, can be perverted to serve selfish and dishonorable purposes. So we are called on to mortify [put to death] the deeds of the body. (Romans 8:13) and not to yield our members as

instruments of unrighteousness unto sin. (6:13) We are to present our bodies to God so that all their ransomed powers can be used for His service under the controlling power of His Holy Spirit.

These two natures abide side by side in the child of God until the redemption of the body. That will take place when the Lord Jesus Christ appears in the rapture to take His people out of this world. **Beloved, now are we the sons of God, and it doth not yet appear what we shall be: but we know that, when he shall appear, we shall be like him; for we shall see him as he is. (1 John 3:2)** What a day that will be—the rapture and glorification of the saints. But, look what else! John declares, **we shall be like Him. (1 John 3:2)** Sin will be forever banished from the Christian's life. We will be with the Saviour in Heaven. **And there shall in no wise enter into it any thing that defileth, neither whatsoever worketh abomination, or maketh a lie: but they which are written in the Lamb's book of life. (Revelation 21:27)** God's desire for every believer will be realized at last. The glorification of the Christian. **For whom he did foreknow, he also did predestinate to be conformed to the image of his Son, that he might be the firstborn among many brethren. (Romans 8:29)** When God looked down through time and saw those who would be saved He predestined them to be like His Son. Because God has determined it, someday **we shall be like him; for we shall see him as he is. (1 John 3:2)**

THE CONFLICT

The presence of these two opposing natures creates within the Christian a great conflict. **For the flesh lusteth against the Spirit, and the Spirit against the flesh: and these are contrary the one to the other: so that ye cannot do the things that ye would. (Galatians 5:17)** The word **lusteth** comes from the Greek *"epithymeo"* and means *"to desire, long for, covet."* It speaks of a strong desire. Paul states that the Spirit and the flesh lust **against** each other, meaning they have opposite desires for us. The flesh wants us to sin while the Spirit wants us to live for Christ. Paul goes on to say that **these are contrary the one to the other.** The word **contrary** means to *"oppose or confront."* Here is the reason for the conflict that Christians have in their life as they struggle to put off the old and put on the new. The flesh dictates that we be one way and the Spirit immediately steps up and opposes the sinful nature and demands that we walk in the Spirit. The same word used here for **contrary** is translated **adversaries** in Luke 13:17 and 1 Corinthians 16:9. An adversary is an enemy or a foe. The flesh and the Spirit are adversaries—they are enemies one of another. They are not going to compromise and will never be at peace. The battle rages as these two adversaries fight to gain ground in the Christian's life.

We must make a decision as to which one of these natures we are going to side with. Our marching orders are from God. Paul said:

> **That ye put off concerning the former conversation the old man, which is corrupt**

> according to the deceitful lusts; And be renewed in the spirit of your mind; And that ye put on the new man, which after God is created in righteousness and true holiness. (Ephesians 4:22-24)

Paul also commanded the Colossian believers to:

> ... **put off all these; anger, wrath, malice, blasphemy, filthy communication out of your mouth. Lie not one to another, seeing that ye have put off the old man with his deeds; And have put on the new man, which is renewed in knowledge after the image of him that created him. (Colossians 3:8-10)**

In the terminology of putting off and putting on Paul compared the Christian life to stripping off the filthy clothes of a sinful past and putting on the white robes of Christ's righteousness. This is a radical change. Jesus said, **That which is born of the flesh is flesh; and that which is born of the Spirit is spirit. (John 3:6)** With two opposing natures abiding in one body there is a constant war going on. That which is born of the flesh is flesh and will always be flesh while we are in this body and therefore, always drawn in the direction of depravity. However, that which is born of the Spirit is spirit and desires to go in the opposite direction of the flesh. Hence, the greatest battle of the Christian life.

THE CONQUEST

This I say then, Walk in the Spirit, and ye shall not fulfil the lust of the flesh. (Galatians 5:16) Here we have the clear command of God to **walk in the Spirit**. The Christian life is often spoken of as a pilgrimage as we are traveling from earth to Heaven. The word **walk** in Scripture, is many times synonymous with lifestyle. A good example is when the Pharisees questioned Jesus, **Then the Pharisees and scribes asked him, Why walk not thy disciples according to the tradition of the elders, but eat bread with unwashen hands?. (Mark 7:5)** The disciples lifestyle was not in keeping with the tradition of the Pharisees. So, to speak of one's walk is to speak of his lifestyle or testimony. **There is therefore now no condemnation to them which are in Christ Jesus, who walk not after the flesh, but after the Spirit. (Romans 8:1)** Paul's instruction to **walk in the Spirit** is a command to live under the Holy Spirit's influence and control as a continual way of life. This is the whole idea of the filling of the Spirit. **And be not drunk with wine, wherein is excess; but be filled with the Spirit. (Ephesians 5:18)** To be filled with the Holy Spirit does not mean that we have more of the Spirit. When we are saved we are indwelt by the Spirit of God. All Christians have the Holy Spirit living in them, **Now if any man have not the Spirit of Christ, he is none of his. (Romans 8:9)** The filling of the Spirit means that He gets more of us at His will. We must yield ourselves to Him allowing Him to take over and control us. The Galatians were living in the flesh instead of the Spirit.

Jesus gave us the Holy Spirit to empower us to walk for and serve Him. **I send the promise of my Father upon you: but tarry ye in the city of Jerusalem, until ye be endued with power from on high. (Luke 24:49)** It is the Spirit of God that furnishes the power to live the Christian life. **Not by might, nor by power, but by my spirit, saith the LORD of**

hosts. (Zechariah 4:6) Jesus said earlier, **It is the spirit that quickeneth; the flesh profiteth nothing: the words that I speak unto you, they are spirit, and they are life. (John 6:63)**

Paul's command is to **walk in the Spirit**. Obeying that command would settle the matter of walking in the flesh vs. walking in the Spirit. The text is clear! If we do walk in the Spirit we will not **fulfil the lust of the flesh**. We by our will and choice decide the course of conduct we will take. You can decide right now which force will rule in your life. Herein lies the means of victory! **WALK IN THE SPIRIT.**

The Works Of The Flesh
Galatians 5:19-22

Now the works of the flesh are manifest... (Galatians 5:19a) Keep in mind that the **flesh** refers to the depraved fallen nature of man. The flesh speaks of what a man is apart from God. The word **manifest** comes from the Greek *"phaneros"* and means *"apparent, open, visible, exposed."* What a man is in his heart will be exposed and visible in his life. The way to identify the flesh is by its works. The product being produced identifies the root source and its condition. Paul identifies four categories of sin that are produced by the flesh.

SINS OF IMMORALITY

Now the works of the flesh are manifest, which are these; Adultery, fornication, uncleanness, lasciviousness, (Galatians 5:19) In this first category Paul lists four sins of immorality. They include Adultery, fornication, uncleanness, and lasciviousness.

The Sin Of Adultery

Adultery is sexual unfaithfulness to a husband or a wife. Noah Webster defines it as *"violation of the marriage bed."* It is the wicked and vile behavior that is regularly practiced and even flaunted in our day. Although this wicked world rejects it, the Word of God is still plain and up to date on this and all matters. The physical relationship between a man and a woman is lawful and honorable only within the bond of marriage. **Marriage is honourable in all, and the bed undefiled: but whoremongers and adulterers God will**

judge. (Hebrews 13:4) The bed is undefiled only for those who are married. God classifies all others as **whoremongers and adulterers**. The Bible is unmistakably clear on this.

Adultery does not have to be an outward physical act. It can also be a secret hidden sin of the heart. **Ye have heard that it was said by them of old time, Thou shalt not commit adultery: But I say unto you, That whosoever looketh on a woman to lust after her hath committed adultery with her already in his heart. (Matthew 5:27-28)** Many who have not committed adultery physically have done so emotionally. However, lets add that by God's grace adultery is forgivable. The Samaritan adulteress was forgiven, saved, and used of God to reach a city for Christ (John 4). Jesus said to the woman taken in adultery, **Neither do I condemn thee: go, and sin no more. (John 8:11)** It is without question that adultery, whether physically and outwardly or committed inwardly and secretly, is a work of the flesh and is a characteristic of an unsaved person.

The Sin Of Fornication

Fornication comes from the word, *"porneia"* and speaks of unlawful sexual activity. It describes sexual immorality in general. It includes sex outside of marriage, incest, sodomy, and lesbianism. Paul says that one who habitually practices this sin will not go to Heaven. **Fornicators ...shall not inherit the kingdom of God. (1 Corinthians 6:9)** A child of God has no business involved in such sin.

> **Flee fornication. Every sin that man doeth is without the body; but he that committeth fornication sinneth against his own body. (1 Corinthians 6:18)**

> But fornication, and all uncleanness, or covetousness, let it not be once named among you, as becometh saints. (Ephesians 5:3)
>
> For this is the will of God, even your sanctification, that ye should abstain from fornication. (1 Thessalonians 4:3)

Fornication is a work of the flesh and absolutely forbidden by God. The Christian is commanded to stay clear of fornication.

The Sin Of Uncleanness

Uncleanness is the opposite of clean and pure. It comes from the Greek *"akatharsia"* and was a medical term that referred to an infected and oozing sore. It is used here to describe the unsaved man whose heart is infected and oozing with sin. **Unto the pure all things are pure: but unto them that are defiled and unbelieving is nothing pure; but even their mind and conscience is defiled. (Titus 1:15)** It describes the filthiness of heart that defiles a person and permeates his life. **I speak after the manner of men because of the infirmity of your flesh: for as ye have yielded your members servants to uncleanness and to iniquity unto iniquity; even so now yield your members servants to righteousness unto holiness. (Romans 6:19)** Uncleanness is a production of the flesh and characteristic of the unsaved.

The Sin Of Lasciviousness

Lasciviousness means *"looseness; irregular indulgence of animal desires; wantonness; lustfulness."* According to Vine's Expository Dictionary, the prominent idea is *"shameless conduct."* It refers to those who have absolutely no shame for the wicked acts they commit. It is a word that speaks of living without restraint or shame. It clearly describes today's society.

SINS OF IDOLATRY

The sins specifically mentioned in this category are **idolatry** and **witchcraft. (Galatians 5:20a)**

The Sin Of Idolatry

Idolatry is the use of idols, images and other substitutes for God. God's people are forbidden to use idols.

> **Thou shalt not make unto thee any graven image, or any likeness of any graven image, or any likeness of any thing that is in heaven above, or that is in the earth beneath, or that is in the water under the earth. Thou shalt not bow down thyself to them, nor serve them: for I the LORD thy God am a jealous God, visiting the iniquity of the fathers upon the children unto the third and fourth generation of them that hate me. (Exodus 20:4-5)**

John commanded:

> **Little children, keep yourselves from idols. Amen. (1 John 5:21)**

An idolater is anyone who does not give Almighty God first place in his life. **Thou shalt love the Lord thy God with all thy heart, and with all thy soul, and with all thy mind. This is the first and great commandment. (Matthew 22:37-38)** We think of idols as statues and images and that is true. However, it goes much further than that. An idol is anything that takes the place of God in your life. It could be your work, food, books, education, possessions, television, or fashion. Your family can be an idol. Anything that squeezes God out is an idol. People idolize ball players, Hollywood stars, musicians, and other worldly people. Many people worship money. If the average Christian would seek after God the way they do things and riches we would have a revival that would shake the world.

The Sin Of Witchcraft

Witchcraft is from the word *"pharmakeia"* and means *"medication, the use or administration of drugs."* Our English *"pharmacy"* is derived from this word. It includes all forms of attempting to control others including administering drugs, horoscopes, casting spells, fortune telling, astrology, palm reading, seances, and other forms of witchcraft. The magicians and witches used drugs to gain control over people. Mark Bubeck ties it into today's drug culture. The use of drugs for sensational, mind-expanding experience is a form of sorcery.

SINS OF INDIFFERENCE

Paul goes on ... **hatred, variance, emulations, wrath, strife, seditions, heresies, Envyings, murders... (Galatians 5:20b-21a)** Here is a list of sins that we see often in our day.

The Sin Of Hatred

Hatred carries the idea of enmity. It is the opposite of love. It speaks of hostility and animosity towards others. It is the kind of hatred that lingers, reproduces. It is a deep rooted and vicious anger. Hatred for others is not acceptable in the Christian life. **He that saith he is in the light, and hateth his brother, is in darkness even until**

now. (1 John 2:9) Love for the brethren is proof of salvation, while hatred is proof that one is lost. The Bible condemns such hatred and places it on the same level with murder. **Whosoever hateth his brother is a murderer: and ye know that no murderer hath eternal life abiding in him. (1 John 3:15)** Hatred for others is proof of a lack of love for God. **If a man say, I love God, and hateth his brother, he is a liar: for he that loveth not his brother whom he hath seen, how can he love God whom he hath not seen?. (1 John 4:20)**

The Sin Of Variance

Variance is strife, discord, contention, fighting, struggling, quarreling, dissension, wrangling. Unfortunately this a prevalent sin toddy. Families are being ripped apart, Churches are being destroyed and society as a whole is miserable because of the sin of variance. Pride is the driving force behind the sin of variance. Solomon said, **Only by pride cometh contention ... (Proverbs 13:10)**

The Sin Of Emulations

Emulations is jealousy. It is wanting and desiring to have what someone else has. It may be position, promotion, property, privilege, or prestige. **Emulations** are manifested as a constant desire to outrival other people to get the admiration and loyalty of others. **For jealousy is the rage of a man: therefore he will not spare in the day of vengeance. (Proverbs 6:34)**

The Sin Of Wrath

Wrath carries the idea of swelling with anger. It is a boiling anger and a raging resentment. Earl White said, *"It derives from a desire of the flesh to strike out at anything* *that threatens self interests."* It is a desire to take vengeance out of the hands of God. The Bible has many warnings against anger. **Wherefore, my beloved brethren, let every man be swift to hear, slow to speak, slow to wrath: for the wrath of man worketh not the righteousness of God. (James 1:19-20)** Strife and turmoil abound in the life of an angry man. **An angry man stirreth up strife, and a furious man aboundeth in transgression. (Proverbs 29:22)** Anger, whether explosive or restrained, is a work of the flesh and carries serious consequences in one's life. Solomon warned, **Be not hasty in thy spirit to be angry: for anger resteth in the bosom of fools (Ecclesiastes 7:9)**

The Sin Of Strife

Strife comes from the Greek *"eritheia"* and speaks of contention and discord that comes from a spirit of self-seeking rivalry. Renn says, *"The sense of 'selfish ambition' is indicated in Phil. 2:3; Jas. 3:14, 16, emphasizing that such an attitude causes disunity and discord among believers."* It speaks of a competitive, factious and striving spirit motivated by a selfish, self-serving, self-seeking attitude. It describes the sin that forces others to choose sides and results in the forming of little cliques and factions. **Let nothing be done through strife or vainglory; but in lowliness of mind let each esteem other better than themselves. (Philippians 2:3)**

The Sin Of Seditions

Seditions is from the word *"dichostasia"* and means *"dividing or splitting."* It carries the idea of division and splitting off from others. This is the wicked sin that has split many churches, marriages and friendships. A seditious person will seek the loyalty of others by dividing them from the ones they are supposed to be loyal to. This is a dangerous work of the flesh. The only way to deal with a seditious person is by marking them and staying away from them. **Now I beseech you, brethren, mark them which cause divisions and offences contrary to the doctrine which ye have learned; and avoid them. (Romans 16:17)**

The Sin Of Heresies

Heresies is that which stands against or opposite of the truth of God. It refers to teachings that are contrary to the Word of God. The word **heresies** comes from a word that means, *"choosing, choice, that which is chosen, or one following his own doctrine."* Noah Webster says, *"An opinion held in opposition to the established or commonly received doctrine..."* Heresy is making a choice to believe and hold to some teaching other than the established truth of God's Word. Churches are setting full of heretics today. They have gathered their opinions from liberal Churches, books, radio preachers, and even Bible college classrooms. Their creeds are nothing more than the teaching of some man. Jesus spoke of this crowd. **But in vain they do worship me, teaching for doctrines the commandments of men. (Matthew 15:9)** Peter warned us that they were coming and would infiltrate the Church. **But there were false prophets also among the people, even as there shall be false teachers among you, who privily shall bring in damnable heresies, even denying the Lord that bought them, and bring upon themselves swift destruction. (2 Peter 2:1)** A heretic is dangerous and must be dealt with. **A man that is an heretick after the first and second admonition reject; (Titus 3:10))**

The Sin Of Envyings

Envyings is a word that is close to emulations, but it goes a step further. Not only is it a jealously that wants what someone else has, but resents the fact that the other person has it. Paul warned us to, **be content with such things as ye have. (Hebrews 13:5)**

The Sin Of Murders

Murder is the premeditated killing of another person. Murder carries severe consequences. **Whoso sheddeth man's blood, by man shall his blood be shed: for in the image of God made he man. (Genesis 9:6)** This is a sin that can be committed inwardly as well as outwardly. There are many Christians who would never take a life physically who are none the less guilty of murder. **Whosoever hateth his brother is a murderer. (1 John 3:15a)**

SINS OF INTEMPERANCE

Drunkenness is the result of using strong drink. America is saturated with wicked drink and drugs. The poison of strong drink has starved more children; wrecked more lives, destroyed more homes; ruined more young people; filled more graves; and sent more people to Hell than any other sin! Strong drink is clearly off limits for the Christian. Only a fool would drink. **Wine is a mocker, strong drink is raging: and whosoever is deceived thereby is not wise. (Proverbs 20:1)**

Revellings speak of merry-making; wild partying; carousing; indulgence, and unlawful pleasure. It is interesting that this word **revellings** is a word that identifies with nocturnal activity—that which is done in the dark or at nighttime. Thayer defines it as:

> "...nocturnal and riotous procession of half drunken and frolicsome fellows who after supper parade through the streets with torches and music in honour of Bacchus or some other deity, and sing and play before houses of male and female friends; hence used generally of feasts and drinking parties that are protracted till late at night and indulge in revelry."

We live in a pleasure drunk society. Even the Churches were filled with pleasure mongers who could take a lesson or two from Moses who chose, **rather to suffer affliction with the people of God, than to enjoy the pleasures of sin for a season. (Hebrews 11:25)** The Bible does not condemn enjoying life and even having fun. It does, however, condemn living for that purpose alone. Jesus said, **And this is the condemnation, that light is come into the world, and men loved darkness rather than light, because their deeds were evil. (John 3:19)**

Paul goes on to say **and such like** indicating that he had not given an exhaustive listing of the works and sins of the flesh. There are others, but the list of seventeen given is surely enough to identify whether or not one is walking in the flesh or in the power of the Spirit.

The Fruit Of The Spirit
Galatians 5:22-26

Having identified the sin that results when we follow the flesh, Paul goes on to list nine virtues that are produced as the Christian yields to the Holy Spirit.

THE CONTRIBUTOR OF THE FRUIT

These Christian virtues are not produced by the efforts of the flesh and they have nothing to do with the abilities of the natural man. The natural man can do nothing to please God. **For I know that in me (that is, in my flesh,) dwelleth no good thing: for to will is present with me; but how to perform that which is good I find not. (Romans 7:18)** All the flesh can produce is wickedness.

This fruit however, is the outworking of the indwelling Holy Spirit as He reigns in the believer's life. Fruit is an outward manifestation of inward life. Fruit is always produced **after his kind** (Genesis 1:11-12, 21-25; 6:20: 7:14). This is an unchangeable law of God. Just as the fruit on a tree is developed by the life in that tree, the fruit of the Spirit is produced by the Holy Spirit.

THE CHARACTERISTICS OF THE FRUIT

But the fruit of the Spirit is love, joy, peace, longsuffering, gentleness, goodness, faith, Meekness, temperance: against such there is no law. (Galatians 5:22-23) As we look at this list, notice that this **fruit** is singular. It is fruit, not fruits. This is a cluster of nine virtues produced by the Spirit in those who walk in the Spirit. This fruit can be divided into three categories:

1) **Upward** toward God — **love, joy, peace**.

2) **Outward** toward others — **longsuffering, gentleness**, and **goodness**.

3) **Inward** toward ourselves — **faith, meekness,** and **temperance**.

Lehman Strauss said:

> "How refreshing just to read these Christian virtues as they stand arrayed against the vices of the flesh."

Robert Gromacki said:

> "The connective "but" (de) shows the contrast between "the works of the flesh" and "the fruit of the Spirit." Works have their source in self, whereas fruit originates from the Spirit. Works manifest what a person does, whereas fruit declares what a man is. Works show conduct, but fruit reveals character. In works the emphasis is on doing, but in fruit the stress is on being."

The Fruit Of Love

Love heads up the list. The fruit of the Spirit is love because **God is love. (1 John 4:8b)**

The Demonstration Of Love

The word **love** comes from "*agape*." It is Calvary love—a self-sacrificing love that gives itself for the person loved. It is the kind of love that demands something of us. The supreme measure and example of *"agape"* love is God's love for sinners. **For God so loved the world, that he gave his only begotten Son, that whosoever believeth in him should not perish, but have everlasting life. (John 3:16)** The greatest demonstration of love this world has ever known is the cross of Calvary. The evidence of His unwavering love is the sacrifice of His Son for the sin of a lost world. **But God commendeth his love toward us, in that, while we were yet sinners, Christ died for us. (Romans 5:8)** Christ's death demonstrated God's unconditional love for us. Calvary's cross is the undeniable proof of God's love.

The next great demonstration of genuine love is the brethren's love for one another. **Beloved, let us love one another: for love is of God; and every one that loveth is born of God, and knoweth God. He that loveth not knoweth not God; for God is love. (1 John 4:7-8)** Our compassion for others, especially for the brethren, is the greatest proof of our salvation. **A new commandment I give unto you, That ye love one another; as I have loved you, that ye also love one another. By this shall all men know that ye are my disciples, if ye have love one to another. (John 13:34-35)** Our love and care of one another gives the lost world a picture of God's love for them.

The Demands Of Love

Hereby perceive we the love of God, because he laid down his life for us: and we ought to lay down our lives for the brethren. (1 John 3:16) The demands of Biblical love go far beyond mere lip service. **But whoso hath this world's good, and seeth his brother have need, and shutteth up his**

bowels of compassion from him, how dwelleth the love of God in him?. (1 John 3:17) True Biblical love knows no boundaries—it is a sacrificial love. When the Holy Spirit has control of our lives He reproduces that same love in us. **The love of God is shed abroad in our hearts by the Holy Ghost which is given unto us. (Romans 5:5b)**

The Division Of Love

There are far too many Christians who are using the excuse of love to be unequally yoked. Paul said, **Let love be without dissimulation. Abhor that which is evil; cleave to that which is good. (Romans 12:9)** Certainly we are to be loving, the Bible is clear on that, but it must be **love ... without dissimulation**. Paul spoke of **love unfeigned. (2 Corinthians 6:6)** Peter used the same terminology. **Seeing ye have purified your souls in obeying the truth through the Spirit unto unfeigned love of the brethren, see that ye love one another with a pure heart fervently: (1 Peter 1:22)** The words **dissimulation** and **unfeigned** come from the same Greek word. It is the word from which we get the English *"hypocrite."* God is telling us to be sincere and genuine in our Christian love. In secular Greek the word hypocrite was an acting term. It spoke of someone who simply played a part. Paul is warning us here not to be an actor playing a part, but to make sure that our love is genuine.

Paul says, **Abhor that which is evil ... (Romans 12:9)** Biblical love demands separation. The word **abhor** comes from the Greek *"apostygeo"* and means *"to hate and detest utterly."* Vine defines **abhor** as meaning *"to render foul* and *to turn oneself away from."* We are to hate and separate from evil.

We are to **cleave to that which is good. (Romans 12:9c)** Biblical love is lived out in one's life. Here is the positive aspect of Biblical separation. We **cleave to that which is good**. When we practice true Bible love, we hate what God hates and we love what God loves. Love divides us from wickedness and unto God.

The question is often asked, "Should we separate from a believer who is not walking with the Lord?" Amos asked, **Can two walk together, except they be agreed? (Amos 3:3)** The Spirit-filled believer has nothing in common with those who walk in the flesh. The Bible clearly commands the believer to separate from other believers who are in error. The Lord Jesus Christ in Matthew 18:15-17 says concerning a **brother** (that's a Christian) who has trespassed against us, **let him be unto thee as a heathen man and a publican**. The heathens and publicans were the most despised and detested people of Jesus' day. To deal with another Christian in such a way would be to separate from him. This is instruction from Jesus Himself concerning separation.

When Paul wrote to the Corinthians dealing with problems in the church at Corinth, he addressed the issue of separation from the brethren. **But now I have written unto you not to keep company, if any man that is called a brother be a fornicator, or covetous, or an idolater, or a railer, or a drunkard, or an extortioner; with such an one no not to eat. (1 Corinthians 5:11)** Notice it says this man is called a **brother** and they were distinctly told **not to keep** company with him. Again Paul says, **Now we command you, brethren, in the name of our Lord Jesus Christ, that ye withdraw yourselves from every brother that walketh disorderly, and not after the tradition which he received of us. (2 Thessalonians 3:6)** Notice that this is not a matter of immorality as in 1st Corinthians, No! This is a matter of conduct. Christian or not, we are not to fellowship with anyone who is not in fellowship with God. Not only is it right to separate from disorderly Christians, it is a command.

The Decision Of Love

Love is a choice—you will personally decide whether or not you will love the Lord. The Church of Ephesus serves an example here. The word Ephesus means desired. Ephesus was a desirable Church. The early churches were the beginning of an eternal plan and purpose. The Church of Ephesus was started by the Apostle Paul. It had begun with great fire and was marked by its missionary and evangelistic zeal, as well as its uncompromising stand for the truth. The Church of Ephesus was **Fundamental**, **Fiery**, **Faithful**, and **Fruitful**—it had been a desirable Church.

They began with a great love for Christ, truth, and a burning desire to see souls saved, but toward the end of the first century she had begun to cool off. The same thing is happening to hordes of Churches across this land. Churches that once stood tall and strong for the things of God have abandoned the old-time religion and died.

The Church of Ephesus had not compromised as of yet. They had, however, taken the first step to compromise and ruin. Jesus said to them, **Nevertheless I have somewhat** against thee, because thou hast left thy first love. (Revelation 2:4)** The love here is described as the **first love**. It is the honeymoon love of the newlywed. Jeremiah calls it the love of the espousal. **Thus saith the LORD; I remember thee, the kindness of thy youth, the love of thine espousals, when thou wentest after me in the wilderness, in a land that was not sown. (Jeremiah 2:2)** Israel is pictured here as the loving bride who clings to her beloved bridegroom. Honeymoon love! The most intimate and cherished love between the bride and groom. It is a time of absolute devotion one to another. Notice the phrase used here, **….the love of thine espousals, when thou wentest after me in the wilderness**. It speaks of the wilderness wanderings when God's people were separated from Egypt and totally dependent on God. This is the love that Jesus wants and deserves.

They had a lot of things right, but the most important thing was out of order—their love of Christ. One preacher of old use to say, People can be straight as a gun barrel theologically, and as empty as a gun barrel spiritually. This statement sums up the condition of the First Baptist Church of Ephesus. They were straight, but they were empty. Jesus didn't charge them with losing their first love, He charged them with leaving their first love.

The Church of Ephesus was getting the job done. But, regardless of the Ephesians great accomplishments, they had failed in their most important task. Jesus said, **Thou shalt love the Lord thy God with all thy heart, and with all thy soul, and with all thy mind. (Matthew 22:37)** No matter what else we may accomplish, when we fail in loving our

Lord with all our heart—we fail most miserably. There is not a more dangerous Christian than one who is operating in the flesh. We must discipline our lives in such a way as to love God with all of our heart. He must be first in our life.

The Fruit Of Joy

Joy is an inner contentment produced by God that is not dependent upon external circumstances. Joy and happiness are not necessarily one and the same. The Christians joy is connected to several things.

First, the **_Possession Of Salvation_**. Happiness is based upon circumstances, joy is based upon a condition. Joy comes from a right relationship with God. **I will greatly rejoice in the LORD, my soul shall be joyful in my God; for he hath clothed me with the garments of salvation, he hath covered me with the robe of righteousness, as a bridegroom decketh himself with ornaments, and as a bride adorneth herself with her jewels. (Isaiah 61:10)** Isaiah was not rejoicing because he had money, a nice house, the latest fashion, or good health. His rejoicing was based upon the fact that he was clothed in the **garments of salvation.** He was a saved man. Too many believers sit around looking like God died and they just got back from the funeral. Why? Because there isn't enough money in the account, they don't have the latest fashion, or their neighbor has a better car. Many Christians allow circumstances to ruin their joy.

Our joy is not dependent on whether or not the bills are paid. It's nice when they are paid and we can praise God for it, but that is not the reason for our rejoicing. We do not rejoice because our health is good and everything seems to be going well. We should be thankful and rejoice over these things, but they are not the basis of our joy. These are all circumstances and circumstances change. If we live for these things and base our joy on them we will change when they change. Instead our joy is based upon our relationship with the Unchangeable Rock of our salvation. God said, **For I am the LORD, I change not. (Malachi 3:6)** This world can crumble and tumble, the stars can fall from the sky, the stock market can crash, and God stands unshakable. We rejoice in spite of circumstances whether they are good or bad because we are God's people. If you are not saved you have nothing to rejoice about—if you are saved you have everything to rejoice about.

Second, the **Presence Of The Saviour. Thou wilt show me the path of life: in thy presence is fulness of joy; at thy right hand there are pleasures for evermore. (Psalm 16:11)** Here we have the Christian's Salvation, Jubilation, and Foundation. There is Path of Salvation, Presence of the Saviour and the Permanence of Satisfaction. We need to notice three important things here. One, real joy can only be realized by God's people. **Thou wilt show me the path of life**. Two, joy is found only in His presence. David said, **in thy presence is fulness of joy**. Three, it is not simply joy, but the **fulness of joy**. Some Christians have joy, but not fullness of joy.

Third, the **Purity Of The Saint. Restore unto me the joy of thy salvation. (Psalm 51:12)** One of the biggest reasons for the Christian's lack of joy is unconfessed and unforsaken sin. In Psalm 51 David was seeking a restored relationship with

God. David had walked with God in the past, but his sin had separated him. He had committed adultery, had Uriah killed, and was still attempting to cover his sin. David learned a hard lesson. You can be successful as a hypocrite for a while, but you mark it down, nothing can be hid from Almighty God. God sent Nathan to deal with David and he repented and sought God's forgiveness. Having been brought face to face with his sin David approached God on the only grounds acceptable—His mercy.

> **Have mercy upon me, O God, according to thy lovingkindness: according unto the multitude of thy tender mercies blot out my transgressions. Wash me thoroughly from mine iniquity, and cleanse me from my sin. For I acknowledge my transgressions: and my sin is ever before me. (Psalm 51:1-3)**

These were the words of a broken man—a man who needed something from God. Notice that David could not walk with God as long as there was sin in his life. **Can two walk together, except they be agreed. (Amos 3:3)** My friend, you mark it down, God does not agree with sin and will deal with it. **But your iniquities have separated between you and your God, and your sins have hid his face from you, that he will not hear. (Isaiah 59:2)** David's sin had cost him his communion with God, but it cost him his joy also. David prayed, **Restore unto me the joy of thy salvation. (Psalm 51:12)** Only after forgiveness and restoration could David experience joy again. Sin had severed his walk with God. He was still saved, but he had lost his joy. Many Christians today are in the same fix.

Fourth, the **_Practice Of The Scriptures_**. **If ye keep my commandments, ye shall abide in my love; even as I have kept my Father's commandments, and abide in his love. These things have I spoken unto you, that my joy might remain in you, and that your joy might be full. (John 15:10-11)** A remaining and full joy is what Jesus wants for every Christian. The word **full** is from the Greek word *"pleroo"* and means to be completely full, lacking nothing. However, such joy is dependent upon obedience to the Word of God. Do you know why some people are miserable? They do not obey God. Obedience to His word is a condition of joy.

Fifth, the **_Perception Of Service_**. To have joy we must be able to see beyond present circumstances. The Apostle Paul while sitting in a Roman prison awaiting execution for preaching the gospel, wrote to the Philippian Church, **Yea, and if I be offered upon the sacrifice and service of your faith, I joy, and rejoice with you all. (Philippians 2:17)** Sacrifice in service will reveal the true state of a man's heart like no other test. The word **offered** refers to the drink offering of the Levitical sacrifices. Paul used the same word when writing to Timothy. **For I am now ready to be offered, and the time of my departure is at hand. (2 Timothy 4:6)** Paul was using this figure of speech to describe his own martyrdom. Paul found great joy in being poured out like a drink offering for the cause of Christ. His life had been sacrificed to God for the purpose of reaching others with the gospel. Now, even in death, he would die sacrificially and joyfully to the glory of Christ. Paul was joyful, even when his execution was imminent, because his perception of service was right. His focus was not himself, but his Christ. The Apostle Paul was a man who continually suffered for the cause of Christ, yet he remained joyful. **Great is my boldness of speech toward you, great is my glorying of you: I am filled with comfort, I am exceeding joyful in all our tribulation. (2 Corinthians 7:4)**

Sometimes in the heat of battle, when the enemy is unloading everything he has at us, it is easy to get our mind off of Christ and on ourselves. However, we must keep the right perspective in service. We are winners in Jesus Christ. He has already, **spoiled principalities and powers, he made a show of them openly, triumphing over them in it. (Colossians 2:15)** The Christianity of the Bible is not a peaches-and-cream religion. We are, however, commanded to, **Rejoice evermore. (1 Thessalonians 5:16)** You say, Preacher, how do we respond in difficult circumstances? We rejoice! **Blessed are ye, when men shall revile you, and persecute you, and shall say all manner of evil against you falsely, for my sake. Rejoice, and be exceeding glad: for great is your reward in heaven: for so persecuted they the prophets which were before you. (Matthew 5:11-12)**

The Fruit Of Peace

Peace is the tranquility of mind that comes from a right relationship with Christ. Like joy, peace is not affected by circumstances. Peace is the opposite of worry and the believer can have the **... peace of God, which passeth all understanding. (Philippians 4:7)** There is big difference between having peace with God and in having the peace of God. One delivers us from His wrath, the other delivers us from the worry. The first comes by trusting Him for our salvation and the second comes from trusting Him in our daily walk.

First, there is a **_Positional Peace_**. This is peace with God. **Therefore being justified by faith, we have peace with God through our Lord Jesus Christ. (Romans 5:1)** Our peace with God is based upon our salvation in Jesus Christ. Apart from salvation no man can be at peace with God.

> **But the wicked are like the troubled sea, when it cannot rest, whose waters cast up mire and dirt. There is no peace, saith my God, to the wicked. (Isaiah 57:20-21)**

The lost man is an enemy of God and there can be no peace between the two except by the atoning work of Christ. **For there is one God, and one mediator between God and men, the man Christ Jesus. (1 Timothy 2:5)**

Second, there is **_Practical Peace_**. This is the peace of God. A lot of people have peace with God because they are saved, but fail in having the peace of God. **Peace with God** is the result of trusting Christ for salvation. **Peace of God** is the result of trusting Him in our daily walk. This is the peace of the overcomer. Jesus said, **These things I have spoken unto you, that in me ye might have peace. In the world ye shall have tribulation: but be of good cheer; I have overcome the world. (John 16:33)** Robert Gromacki said:

> "This peace is a legacy of Christ, totally foreign to the experience of the world (John 14:27). It is that inner calmness of emotions and thoughts which rests on the assurance that God is too good

to be unkind and too wise to make mistakes."

This is the Spirit produced peace that manifests in the believer who is totally surrendered to and trusting Christ no matter what is happening in his life. No matter our circumstances we have certainty and assurance that God is in control.

> **And we know that all things work together for good to them that love God, to them who are the called according to *his* purpose. (Romans 8:28)**

Jesus said, **Peace I leave with you, my peace I give unto you: not as the world giveth, give I unto you. Let not your heart be troubled, neither let it be afraid. (John 14:27)** Because our peace is not affected by circumstances we can have peace in every situation. **Great peace have they which love thy law: and nothing shall offend them. (Psalm 119:165)**

The Fruit Of Longsuffering

The word **longsuffering** comes from the Greek *"makrothymia"* and means *"forbearance, patience, endurance."* The word carries the idea of restraint and patient endurance of mistreatment without anger or thought of revenge. That is a hard thing to accomplish in the flesh. The flesh seeks revenge. However, when we are under the Spirit's control, He will produce patience and longsuffering in our life.

Longsuffering is a Spirit produced virtue that enables us to put up with people who try our patience. When the flesh says, retaliate, longsuffering says love them. Longsuffering is one of God's attributes. **But thou, O Lord, art a God full of compassion, and gracious, longsuffering, and plenteous in mercy and truth. (Psalm 86:15)** If we live a Spirit filled life we too, will be longsuffering even under mistreatment.

When Jesus hung on the cross He could have summoned **more than twelve legions of angels. (Matthew 26:53)** to His side, instead, **endured the cross. (Hebrews 12:2)** Later He prayed for their forgiveness. **Then said Jesus, Father, forgive them; for they know not what they do. And they parted his raiment, and cast lots. (Luke 23:34)** That is the greatest example of longsuffering.

The Fruit Of Gentleness

Gentleness is from the Greek *"chrestotes"* and means *"useful, profitable. gracious, kind, profitable."* Noah Webster says, *"Genteel behavior. Softness of manners; mildness of temper; sweetness of disposition; meekness."* **Gentleness** is best defined as grace in action. It speaks of a genuine and tender concern for others. It is the genuine desire to treat others with the same grace that our Lord has shown us. Paul practiced this kind of gentleness.

> **But we were gentle among you, even as a nurse cherisheth her children: So being affectionately desirous of you, we were willing to have imparted unto you, not the gospel of God only, but also our own souls, because ye were dear unto us. (1 Thessalonians 2:7-8)**

As Christian workers we need to remember the grace and gentleness with which God dealt with us. Gentleness is a qualification for service. **And the servant of the Lord must** not strive; but be gentle unto all men, apt to teach, patient. (2 Timothy 2:24)** There are a lot of good men and women who have failed in service for Christ, not because they were compromisers, but because they could not keep a balance between truth and grace. Remember, **gentleness** is grace in action.

The Fruit Of Goodness

Goodness is from *"agathosyne"* and speaks of the honesty and integrity of heart that not only despises evil, but refrains from doing it. It is a heart condition that produces a good lifestyle. It is conviction with action. This goodness is a characteristic of God. David said, **I had fainted, unless I had believed to see the goodness of the LORD in the land of the living. (Psalm 27:13)** This same goodness is reproduced in the Christian's life as he yields to the Holy Spirit. It is a quality that we need in dealing with others. **As we have therefore opportunity, let us do good unto all men, especially unto them who are of the household of faith. (Galatians 6:10)**

The Fruit Of Faith

Faith is the virtue that takes God at His Word. It is a God said it and that settles it faith. Faith does not question God. There are no other grounds upon which to approach God. There is no other avenue by which to live the Christian life. It is all of faith and nothing else. **But without faith it is impossible to please him: for he that cometh to God must believe that he is, and that he is a rewarder of them that diligently seek him. (Hebrews 11:6)** God never requires that we understand His plan and purposes, just that we obey him. We need no explanations. **For we walk by faith, not by sight. (2 Corinthians 5:7)** The Bible declares, **The just shall live by faith. (Galatians 3:11b)** This is another word that requires action. It is faith that produces faithfulness. Faith is often tried, but true faith endures regardless of the circumstances. **Knowing this, that the trying of your faith worketh patience. (James 1:3)** The trials and tribulations of this world do not stop the faithful. **So that we ourselves glory in you in the churches of God for your patience and faith in all your persecutions and tribulations that ye endure. (2 Thessalonians 1:4)** The Thessalonian believers had suffered a great deal of persecution for their faith. However, they had faithfully endured the persecution and remained true to God. Jesus said, **be thou faithful unto death, and I will give thee a crown of life. (Revelation 2:10b)** Faith asks no questions, requires no explanations, and fears no consequences—it simply believes and obeys. Faith is not only believing regardless of evidence, it is obeying regardless of consequences.

The Fruit Of Meekness

Meekness is a word that basically means *"mild, gentle, or softness of temper."* Meekness is not weakness or a lack of power. Rather, it is power under control. An ox has tremendous power, but in the yoke is under control and able to be turned in any direction by the will of its master. Jesus is the perfect example of meekness. **Take my yoke upon you, and learn of me; for I am meek and lowly in heart: and ye shall find rest unto your souls. (Matthew 11:29)**

Meekness is also a requirement for reaching people. **In meekness instructing those that oppose themselves; if God peradventure will give them repentance to the acknowledging of the truth. (2 Timothy 2:25)** It is a requirement for restoring the fallen. **Brethren, if a man be overtaken in a fault, ye which are spiritual, restore such an one in the spirit of meekness; considering thyself, lest thou also be tempted. (Galatians 6:1)** Meekness results in the character to control and discipline our self.

The Fruit Of Temperance

Temperance is having control over fleshly desires and impulses. According to Webster it is, *"habitual moderation in regard to the indulgence of the natural appetites and passions."* Paul uses this word in 1 Corinthians 7:9 speaking of controlling sexual desire. He uses it again in 1 Corinthians 9:25 describing the control of an athlete over his desires during training. It carries the idea of self-control. It is having the character and ability to endure temptation without yielding to it. In the context here it is the whole being—body, soul, and spirit under subjection to the Holy Spirit of God.

THE CULTIVATION OF THE FRUIT

After listing the nine characteristics of the Spirit-led Christian Paul says, **against such there is no law. (Galatians 5:23)** These are qualities that cannot be legislated by our own works. Producing acceptable fruit and pleasing God is impossible by works of the flesh. However, by the power of the indwelling Spirit, as we surrender to Him, we can produce good fruit and walk so as to please God.

Our Conversion

And they that are Christ's ... (Galatians 5:24a) There is a distinction made between **they that are Christ's** and they that are not. The believer belongs to God. He is **bought with a price (1 Corinthians 6:20)** Not everyone is a Christian. The liberals teach the Fatherhood of God and the brotherhood of man. There is no such doctrine. To the unsaved, Jesus said, **Ye are of your father the devil. (John 8:44)** One must be born again to be a child of God.

Our Crucifixion

... have crucified the flesh with the affections and lusts. (Galatians 5:24b) The Christian's crucifixion that Paul spoke of earlier is the work of God.

> **I am crucified with Christ: nevertheless I live; yet not I, but Christ liveth in me: and the life which I now live in the flesh I live by the faith of the Son of God, who loved me, and gave himself for me. (Galatians 2:20)**

This is the same crucifixion spoken of in Romans.

> **Knowing this, that our old man is crucified with him, that the body of sin might be destroyed, that henceforth we should not serve sin. (Romans 6:6)**

In these passages the Bible speaks of a definite act of Almighty God in every believer, whereby at the moment of salvation God declares the flesh to be dead. As far as God is concerned every believer's old nature is dead and nailed to the cross. Because of the new birth and the indwelling presence and power of the Holy Spirit, the flesh has been rendered powerless. **Let not sin therefore reign in your mortal body, that ye should obey it in the lusts thereof. (Romans 6:12)**

However, it is important that we realize this crucifixion is also self-inflicted. **And they that are Christ's have crucified the flesh with the affections and lusts. (Galatians 5:24)** This is our personal responsibility. **Likewise reckon ye also yourselves to be dead indeed unto sin, but alive unto God through Jesus Christ our Lord. (Romans 6:11)** God has declared the believer dead in Christ. Now it is our responsibility to **reckon** our own selves dead. We must by faith reckon it to be true in our own life. The word **reckon** comes from the Greek *"logizomai"* and means *"to count, to number, or to calculate."* According to Noah Webster, it carries the idea of *"reasoning with one's self and conclude from arguments."* It is like reconciling a checkbook. We take the bank statement and our checkbook, sit down and make the checkbook agree with the bank statement. That is what God is saying when He commands that we **reckon** ourselves to be dead. He has already declared it. The only thing left is for us to bring our life in line with His word. Reckoning is the step of faith that acknowledges what God says about me in the Bible is true in my life.

Crucifixion is not a pretty or a desirable thing. Crucifixion means death and a horrible one at that. Let's take note of four things about crucifixion.

First, it is a **_Separating_** death. Death separates us from people and places that we love. When the Christian dies to himself he is going to have to say a final goodbye to some people, places, practices, and pleasures that he enjoys in the flesh. Crucifying the flesh it will separate us from our own desires and unto the Lord Jesus Christ.

Second, it is a **_Shameful_** death. Crucifixion was reserved for the most despicable criminals known to man. When a criminal hung on the cross, he hung there under condemnation and in shame for his crimes. A sign was usually hung making known the particular crime or crimes that the condemned man was dying for. It was a shameful situation to be in. To crucify the flesh Christians are going to have to admit that their lifestyle and wickedness is a shameful and criminal offence before Almighty God and separate from it.

Third, it is a **_Suffering_** death. Words cannot began to describe the suffering that took place when one hung for hours on a Calvary's cruel cross. Let us not forget that when Christ hung on Calvary's cross, He suffered under the hand of Almighty God for our sin. He suffered the wrath that we were supposed to receive. Jesus gave up everything to come to this sin infested world and die for us. A lot of Christians will not reckon themselves crucified because it would require too much on their part to forsake this world for Christ. They don't want to suffer the loss of friends, fame, and finances.

Fourth, it is a **_Slow_** death. Sometimes it would take a condemned man days to die as he simply hung on the cross and wasted away moment by moment. It was a slow and agonizing death. Many Christians have tried to reckon themselves dead to sin, but they soon found out that it was a battle. It is a battle that takes time. It is a slow and agonizing conflict. There is nothing pleasant about it. There is no quick fix. However, it is commanded and necessary.

Our Conduct

If we live in the Spirit, let us also walk in the Spirit. (Galatians 5:25) It is for certain that once we are crucified, our conduct changes. In the book of Romans as well as here in Galatians, Paul proclaimed that we are now free from the law and its bondage. His argument is simple. Now that we know Christ we have the Holy Spirit to empower us to live the Christian life. Now we live and walk in the Spirit. Our life is to reflect the fact that sin no longer has bondage over us. Jesus said, **Verily, verily, I say unto you, Whosoever committeth sin is the servant of sin. (John 8:34)** The believer is not a servant of sin, but a servant of Christ. For anyone who will trust His finished work, Christ's death on the cross broke the chains of bondage that enslaves the human race. We must keep in mind that our liberty is freedom from sin, not freedom to sin. This liberty is the freedom we have in Christ to say no to sin and yes to His Spirit. **Stand fast therefore in the liberty wherewith Christ hath made us free, and be not entangled again with the yoke of bondage. (Galatians 5:1)** We are free in Christ never again to be brought into bondage by sin. **For sin shall not have dominion over you: for ye are not under the law, but**

under grace. (Romans 6:14) Since we are no longer slaves to sin we can walk a new course in life.

Our Concern

Let us not be desirous of vain glory, provoking one another, envying one another. (Galatians 5:26) Putting others first is a priority. Paul warned the Philippians on this when he said, **Let nothing be done through strife or vainglory; but in lowliness of mind let each esteem other better than themselves. (Philippians 2:3)** To put others first is a work of the Holy Spirit and is completely contrary to depraved human nature. The sin of being **desirous of vain glory** is a sin which causes a lot of trouble among Christians. The phrase **vain glory** comes from the Greek *"kenodoxos"* and speaks of self-conceit and arrogance. It describes someone who tries to appear as something more than he is. It is like Simon who went around ... **giving out that himself was some great one: (Acts 8:9)** Vain glory is the sin of setting oneself above fellow Christians. It is the sin of over estimating one's self-worth. Paul warned:

> **For I say, through the grace given unto me, to every man that is among you, not to think of himself more highly than he ought to think; but to think soberly, according as God hath dealt to every man the measure of faith. (Romans 12:3)**

The exaltation and praise of self is a pride to the related work of the flesh. In other words, if we are to win we must deal with pride.

Vain glory results in ... **provoking one another, envying one another. (Galatians 5:26)** It is a fleshly work that promotes jealously and envy. It leads to disruption and disunity. It is a sin driven by pride and man thinking more highly of himself than he ought to.

God expects every Christian to be Spirit-filled. One who is filled with the Spirit will exhibit the fruit of the Spirit. We are either walking in the flesh or in the Spirit. The choice is ours. **This I say then, Walk in the Spirit, and ye shall not fulfil the lust of the flesh. (Galatians 5:16)**

The Ministry Of Restoration
Galatians 6:1-6

When General William Booth, the founder of the Salvation Army, was up in years, he was asked to address a large convention of workers and volunteers. But due to his hectic schedule he was unable to attend. Instead he was asked to send a greeting. The message he sent went like this:

> To the delegates of the Salvation Army convention:
>
> Others.
>
> General William Booth

Warren Wiersbe has well said, *"... nothing reveals the wickedness of legalism better than the way the legalists treat those who have sinned."* God's people are to look out for one another.

> **Brethren, if any of you do err from the truth, and one convert him; Let him know, that he which converteth the sinner from the error of his way shall save a soul from death, and shall hide a multitude of sins. (James 5:19-20)**

If a brother or sister falls we are to pick them up and restore them to fellowship. This is the way of the Christian life.

THE POSSIBILITY

Brethren, if a man be overtaken in a fault, (Galatians 6:1a) The word **brethren** is found over two hundred times in the New Testament. It is a term that is applied to those who are born into the family of God. Yes, the tragic possibility of failure does exist. **Wherefore let him that thinketh he standeth take heed lest he fall. (1 Corinthians 10:12)** No believer is a hundred percent fall proof. Here we see that it is possible for a Christian to be **overtaken in a fault.** The word **fault** carries the idea of *"trespassing or crossing the line."* The word **overtaken** comes from the Greek *"prolambano"* and means to be *"caught by."* Sin always catches up with us. Moses said, **… be sure your sin will find you out. (Numbers 32:23)**

These who have been **overtaken** are Christians who fell into sin. They have heard the gospel and have received Christ as Saviour. It is a sad fact that all over the world you can find people who trusted the Lord as their Saviour who have fallen away from the Lord and are forsaken and forgotten by God's people. They used to attended Church. Some preached the word. Others taught in Sunday-School. Some ushered. Some would sing. Many of them had prominent positions in the Church. But they have been overtaken by a fault. Let us not forget that our God is the God of the second chance and he wants erring Christians restored.

THE PREREQUISITE

… ye which are spiritual, (Galatians 6:1b) Here is a requirement for those who want to help the backslider. The job isn't for just anyone, rather, it is for those who are **spiritual**. What does it mean to be spiritual? Paul has already given us the answer. It means that …

1) We are walking by the Spirit (5:16).

2) We are not practicing the works of the flesh (5:19-21).

3) The fruit of the Spirit is evident in our life (5:22-23).

The point is, we cannot restore someone to a Spiritual walk if we are not walking in the Spirit.

THE PROCESS

... restore such an one (Galatians 6:1c) The word **restore** comes from the Greek *"katartizo."* It is a powerful and picturesque word. It carries the idea of *"repairing, mending and returning to a former state."* It was a word that was commonly used for setting broken bones. The word implies care and healing. A broken bone does not heal instantly. The setting of a broken bone requires much wisdom and work. Restoring a fellow believer will involve hard work, care and time. This is where compassion comes in. C. I. Scofield said:

> "Oh! what love and longsuffering and gentleness and meekness and goodness and faith the ministry of restoration requires! It is work, indeed, which taxes the utmost resources of grace.. For no one is so hard to get on with, no one is so critical, so unreasonable, as a saint out of communion. But thank God, love can do it."

This same word *"katartizo,"* is used of **mending** nets (Matthew 4:21). This describes the outcome of restoration. Those nets have failed the fisherman. They had become worn and as a result broke and were unable to hold fish. They were unable to be used in the work because of the condition they were in. They were **overtaken in a fault.** However, the nets were being mended. They weren't being mended so that they could be put on a shelf. Rather, the fisherman were going to put the mended nets back into service. Whether it is putting a broken bone back in place or the mending of fishing nets, the idea is clear! The propose is restoration to service. The fallen can be used of God once restoration has taken place.

THE PRUDENCE

... in the spirit of meekness; (Galatians 6:1d) There is a caution here. We have already learned that meekness is a fruit of the Spirit. To be meek is to be *"mild and gentle."* It does not mean that we are to be a wimp. Jesus was meek, but He stood for truth while at the same time reaching out to the hurting. We must be meek, but at the same time we cannot compromise the truth in order to appeal to the backslider. Let us also remember that it is not our job to punish the erring believer, but to help him up. We are to get him back on his feet and back in God's house.

THE PRECAUTION

... considering thyself, lest thou also be tempted. (Galatians 6:1e) We must take extreme caution when we deal with erring brethren. Every one of us are inclined to the snags and snares of sin. It is easier for us to get drawn into their sin than for us to draw them out. We must be careful.

Bear ye one another's burdens, and so fulfil the law of Christ. (Galatians 6:2) The word **burden** comes from the Greek *"baros."* It carries the idea of being *"weighty or hard to bear."* The word **bear** means to *"support or carry."* Many times people have burdens that are simply too much for them to bear alone.

> **Two *are* better than one; because they have a good reward for their labour. For if they fall, the one will lift up his fellow: but woe to him *that is* alone when he falleth; for *he hath* not another to help him up. (Ecclesiastes 4:9-10)**

Solomon explains that **two are better than one.** Just helping someone bear his load goes a long way. Sometimes that is all a person needs in order to get back in fellowship with the Lord. Helping others bear their load is a major part of the ministry of restoration.

For if a man think himself to be something, when he is nothing, he deceiveth himself. (Galatians 6:3) Many approach the backslider with the attitude of, *"I will never fall into sin."* The Scriptures say, **Wherefore let him that thinketh he standeth take heed lest he fall. (1 Corinthians 10:12)** This is why Paul commanded us not to think more highly of ourselves than we ought (Romans 12:3).

THE PROVING

But let every man prove his own work, and then shall he have rejoicing in himself alone, and not in another. For every man shall bear his own burden. (Galatians 6:4) Paul is still dealing with man in verse 3 who thinks himself to be something. The idea is, if you think you are something—prove it! The word **prove** means *"to examine, put to the test."* It carries the idea of *"discerning, examining, and testing for the purpose of approving."* It was a blacksmith's term for testing so as to approve a piece of metal for its strength. In like manner, Paul calls upon us to examine and test ourselves to be sure that we are what we say we are.

For every man shall bear his own burden. (Galatians 6:5) Some have stumbled at this verse supposing there to be a contradiction between verse two and verse five. In verse 2 Paul said, **Bear ye one another's burdens ...** Here he says, **every man shall bear his own burden.** Rest assured that there is no contradiction here. Verse 2 has to do with helping someone else with their burden while verse 5 has to do with bearing our own responsibility when we stand before Christ at the Judgment Seat.

The Harvest Is Coming
Galatians 6:7-10

In this section Paul introduces the spiritual way of sowing and reaping. This passage is often applied to the lost to warn them their wickedness and their day judgment. While that application can be made, we must realize that the passage was written to God's people. God's people do not escape the consequences of their sin. A day of reckoning is coming and the Christian who thinks that he can play with sin and sow to the flesh will answer to God. Paul's admonitions are serious.

THE DECREED REALITY

Be not deceived; God is not mocked ... (Galatians 6:7a) The word **deceived** comes from the Greek *"planao"* and carries the idea of being seduced and lead astray. It means *"to roam, err, wander, be out of the way."* That is what legalism does. It seduces and leads astray. In the context of the book, legalism leads us away from grace. There are plenty of deceived seducers out there. **But evil men and seducers shall wax worse and worse, deceiving, and being deceived. (2 Timothy 3:13)** The Galatians had been seduced by the Judaizers. So much so that Paul said they were **bewitched. (Galatians 3:1)** They had been duped into roaming away from grace and reverting back to the law.

Added to Paul's warning is the declaration that **God is not mocked.** The word **mocked** comes from *"mykterizo."* it means to *"to turn up one's nose."* It carries the idea of *"making mouth, ridiculing, mocking."* It describes the work of a scorner. Legalist's are good at scorning God's grace. They treat God's grace with contempt and mockery. Paul warns that God is not mocked. A day of reckoning is coming and the record will be set straight.

THE DISTINCTION REAPED

... for whatsoever a man soweth, that shall he also reap. (Galatians 6:7b) This is a spiritual law—we reap what we sow. The phrases, **after his kind** and **after their kind** are used numerous times in Genesis chapter one (Genesis 1:11, 12, 21, 24, 25). It is clearly stated that everything reproduces **after their kind.** The farmer doesn't sow wheat and reap barley. You don't plant an apple tree and get peaches from it. The law of nature is everything reproduces after its own kind. Paul takes the truth of sowing and reaping and illustrates that fact that we will reap a harvest according to our sowing.

For he that soweth to his flesh shall of the flesh reap corruption... (Galatians 6:8a) The flesh speaks of our sinful nature. It is a nature that is an enemy of God and hates everything that is holy and decent. **For I know that in me (that is, in my flesh,) dwelleth no good thing: for to will is present with me; but how to perform that which is good I find not. (Romans 7:18)** It was the old depraved nature that Jeremiah was speaking of when he said, **The heart is deceitful above all things, and desperately wicked: who can know it? (Jeremiah 17:9)** Too many who claim to be believers are operating according the old corrupt nature. Such will be their reaping. **Even as I have seen, they that**

plow iniquity, and sow wickedness, reap the same. (Job 4:8)

…. but he that soweth to the Spirit shall of the Spirit reap life everlasting. (Galatians 6:8b) God's people are not dependent on the Flesh. **Therefore, brethren, we are debtors, not to the flesh, to live after the flesh. (Romans 8:12)** God has given us the Holy Spirit to guide us and empower us to live above the flesh. **This I say then, Walk in the Spirit, and ye shall not fulfil the lust of the flesh. (Galatians 5:16)** Rather than a harvest of corruption, we can reap eternal things after the Spirit. Those who operate according to the Spirit of God will reap eternal things. **With good will doing service, as to the Lord, and not to men: Knowing that whatsoever good thing any man doeth, the same shall he receive of the Lord, whether he be bond or free. (Ephesians 6:7-8)** Not only in this life will we reap according to our sowing, but also beyond the grave. We can be sure that our deeds will follow us into eternity where we will stand before the Just God of Glory and answer to Him.

THE DETERMINATION REWARDED

And let us not be weary in well doing: for in due season we shall reap, if we faint not. (Galatians 6:9) The word **weary** carries the idea of *"fatigue and exhaustion."* It is a spiritual weariness and exertion that leads to one losing heart and giving up. We must stay the course and press toward the mark **… for in due season we shall reap, if we faint not.** The word **faint** carries the idea of *"wearied, exhausted, or to loose heart."* According to Webster, it speaks of being *"weak; feeble; languid; exhausted; as faint* *with fatigue."* The idea is that of a soldier becoming battle weary and surrendering. Notice that our reaping is in **due season.** Not in your season, not in my season, but In **due season**! Again, the analogy of farming is used. The farmer sows his seed, but must wait until the harvest season to reap. Our responsibility is to be faithful in God's work. We know that there will be a harvest in due season.

THE DUTY REQUIRED

As we have therefore opportunity, let us do good unto all men, especially unto them who are of the household of faith. (Galatians 6:10) The word **therefore** shows that Paul is continuing his discussion of the harvest. Because there is a harvest coming and because we will reap according to our sowing, we are to take every **opportunity** to **do good**. Doing good encompasses all that Paul has just taught including bearing one another's burdens, sowing to the Spirit and staying by the stuff. If we will be faithful, the harvest will be fruitful.

Glorying In The Cross
Galatians 6:11-18

As Paul comes to the conclusion of his letter, he gives a brief summation of all that he has said.

THE CONDITION HE FELT

Ye see how large a letter I have written unto you with mine own hand. (Galatians 6:11) The words **large a letter** does not refer to the length of the letter but the size of Paul's handwriting. We know that Paul suffered from poor eyesight. This was probably the **thorn in the flesh** that Paul spoke of (2 Corinthians 12:7). Paul also alluded to it earlier when he told the Galatians, **.. if it had been possible, ye would have plucked out your own eyes, and have given them to me. (Galatians 4:15)** Because of poor eyesight Paul would dictate his letters to an amanuensis. **I Tertius, who wrote this epistle, salute you in the Lord. (Romans 16:22)** Tertius was Paul's secretary. Paul spoke under the inspiration of the Holy Spirit (2 Peter 1:21) and Tertius faithfully transcribed as Paul dictated. Here in Galatians however, Paul penned the letter personally to them. His poor eyesight forced him to write in large letters so that he could see what he was writing.

THE CORRUPTION HE FOUGHT

As many as desire to make a fair shew in the flesh, they constrain you to be circumcised ... (Galatians 6:12a) The phrase **a fair shew in the flesh** describes a good bit of today's religion. It's an outward facade with no inward change. Notice the words, **they constrain you**. The Judaizers held the law over people.

... only lest they should suffer persecution for the cross of Christ. (Galatians 6:12b) Remember that these Judaizers had infiltrated the Church. They had made a profession of faith in Christ. They professed Christ until the lines were drawn and they figured out that it was going to cost them to stay the course. They sided with the legalists lest they should **suffer persecution for the cross of Christ.**

For neither they themselves who are circumcised keep the law; but desire to have you circumcised, that they may glory in your flesh. (Galatians 6:13) The Judaizers weren't following through on the law in their own lives. The Pharisees of Jesus' day were guilty of the same thing.

> **Then spake Jesus to the multitude, and to his disciples, Saying, The scribes and the Pharisees sit in Moses' seat: All therefore whatsoever they bid you observe,** *that* **observe and do; but do not ye after their works: for they say, and do not. For they bind heavy burdens and grievous to be borne, and lay** *them* **on men's shoulders; but they** *themselves* **will not move them with one of their fingers. But all their works they do for to be seen of men: they make broad their phylacteries, and enlarge the borders of their garments, And love the uppermost rooms at feasts, and the chief seats in the synagogues, (Matthew 23:1-6)**

Paul saw the real danger of legalism. Not only were the Judaizers a bunch of self-serving religious crooks, they were sending others to Hell. Let me state once again that a legalist is not someone who has convictions and standards, but one who attempts to make those standards a requisite for salvation. The Judaizers made circumcision a requirement for salvation. Again the Pharisees of Jesus' day serve as an example.

> **But woe unto you, scribes and Pharisees, hypocrites! for ye shut up the kingdom of heaven against men: for ye neither go in *yourselves*, neither suffer ye them that are entering to go in. Woe unto you, scribes and Pharisees, hypocrites! for ye devour widows' houses, and for a pretence make long prayer: therefore ye shall receive the greater damnation. Woe unto you, scribes and Pharisees, hypocrites! for ye compass sea and land to make one proselyte, and when he is made, ye make him twofold more the child of hell than yourselves. (Matthew 23:13-15)**

Legalists always stress the outward things. Ritual and religion are more important to them than salvation and liberty in Christ. Legalist aren't concerned for the real needs of people. They don't care that people are hurting and broken. Their main concern is that they make **a fair shew in the flesh.** Legalism always puts more emphasis to the outward than to the heart. We need to remember that Christians are made from the inside out.

THE CAUSE HE FOSTERED

But God forbid that I should glory, save in the cross of our Lord Jesus Christ, by whom the world is crucified unto me, and I unto the world. (Galatians 6:14) In contrast to the

Judaizers who gloried in the fleshly accomplishments of their own work, Paul gloried in the cross. When Paul wrote about the cross here, he wasn't just speaking of the wooden instrument upon which Christ died. His words go much deeper than mere wood. Paul was speaking of the accomplishment of Christ on the cross. The Apostle was stressing the fact that man's sin was paid for and his salvation purchased at Calvary.

For in Christ Jesus neither circumcision availeth any thing, nor uncircumcision, but a new creature. (Galatians 6:15) Paul states clearly that in Jesus Christ the ritual and regulation of the law accomplishes nothing. The law is powerless to provide for man that which he needs most—the new birth. In the law there is condemnation; but in Christ there is conversion. Those who come to Christ are regenerated. Regeneration is at the core of Christianity. Jesus said, **Verily, verily, I say unto thee, Except a man be born of water and of the Spirit, he cannot enter into the kingdom of God. That which is born of the flesh is flesh; and that which is born of the Spirit is spirit. (John 3:5-6)** This is the regenerating work of the Holy Spirit. **Not by works of righteousness which we have done, but according to his mercy he saved us, by the washing of regeneration, and renewing of the Holy Ghost. (Titus 3:5)** Noah Webster defines **regeneration** as *"Reproduction; the act of producing anew."* Our first birth was the result of a generation from our parents. The second birth is a regeneration whereby we are born again. It is a spiritual birth from the Holy Spirit as He imparts to us new spiritual life and we become **partakers of the divine nature. (2 Peter**

1:4) Paul said, **Therefore if any man be in Christ, he is a new creature: old things are passed away; behold, all things are become new. (2 Corinthians 5:17)**

THE CONCLUSION HE FINALIZES

And as many as walk according to this rule, peace be on them, and mercy, and upon the Israel of God. (Galatians 6:16) The only ones upon whom God's peace and mercy can be bestowed on those who **walk according to this rule.** This is those whose faith is in and on Christ alone for salvation. **Therefore being justified by faith we have peace with God through our Lord Jesus Christ. (Romans 5:1)**

The phrase **Israel of God** draws a contrast between those who were merely born a Jew and Jews who were born again. The true Israelite is one who accepts Jesus as his Messiah. Thus, he speaks of Jewish converts to Christianity as the true **Israel of God.** Paul made the same argument in the book of Romans. ... **For they are not all Israel, which are of Israel: Neither, because they are the seed of Abraham, are they all children: (Romans 9:6b-7a)** Just being born of the seed of Abraham does not make one a true son of Abraham. Paul's argument was that He must have the faith of Abraham.

From henceforth let no man trouble me: (Galatians 6:17a) Paul says, *"I don't want to hear anymore about it. I have shown where you are wrong. I have made myself clear. End of discussion."* Paul wasn't going to waste valuable time and energy debating and arguing with folks who weren't going to change anyway.

... for I bear in my body the marks of the Lord Jesus. **(Galatians 6:17b)** The word **marks** comes from the Greek *"stigma"* and speaks of a permanent scar. It was the word used to describe a brand that was burned into to the flesh of cattle and slaves to signify ownership. The Judaizers were interested in **a fair shew in the flesh**, but Paul points out the scars and marks received from the scourgings, stonings, and shipwrecks.

Of the Jews five times received I forty *stripes* save one. Thrice was I beaten with rods, once was I stoned, thrice I suffered shipwreck, a night and a day I have been in the deep; (2 Corinthians 11:24-25)

Paul was probably contrasting the mark of circumcision with the marks of suffering for Christ. These weren't **a fair show** like the Judaizers gloried in. These were real marks of suffering that Paul had received for preaching the cross of Christ.

The word **bear** comes from the Greek *"bastazo"* and means *"to bear a burden."* It wasn't easy but Paul took his stand and stayed his course. Vance Havner said, *"We have a lot of metals today, but not many scars."* Paul's scars were the marks of his unwavering loyalty to Christ. The Judaizers were big on outward pomp and position, but they had nothing that would endure the fire of judgment.

It will cost us to serve Christ. May God help us to bear the scars to His glory. Polycarp, the bishop of Smyrna, was one of the first martyrs to die for Christ. At 86 years of age they tied him to a stake, piled the wood high and set it afire. As Polycarp was pressured by the Roman proconsul to renounce Christ and be set free, he answered, *"Eighty and six years have I served Him and He never did me any injury. How then can I blaspheme my King and my Savior?"* J. H. Jowett said, *"Ministry that costs nothing, accomplishes nothing."*

Brethren, the grace of our Lord Jesus Christ be with your spirit. Amen. (Galatians 6:18) Grace is the key word in Galatians. Paul addresses the **Brethren**, those who share this special family relationship because of a common faith in Christ. Paul asks for continued grace in their lives.